Swimming Lessons for Baby Sharks:

The Essential Guide to Thriving as a New Lawyer

By

Grover E. Cleveland

WEST®

A Thomson Reuters business

Mat # 40908177

Disclaimer

Anecdotes and examples in this book are based on actual events, but have been modified to more clearly demonstrate particular points and protect the privacy of those involved. Any similarity to actual persons or events is purely coincidental.

Thomson Reuters created this publication to provide you with accurate and authoritative information concerning the subject matter covered. However, this publication was not necessarily prepared by persons licensed to practice law in a particular jurisdiction. Thomson Reuters does not render legal or other professional advice, and this publication is not a substitute for the advice of an attorney. If you require legal or other expert advice, you should seek the services of a competent attorney or other professional.

© 2010 Grover E. Cleveland

Thomson Reuters
610 Opperman Drive
St. Paul, MN 55123
1-800-313-9378

Printed in the United States of America

ISBN: 978-0-314-91747-8

To Foster Pepper PLLC with special thanks
to Steve DiJulio who taught me to practice law
and to Lori Nomura who made it a blast.

How to Use This Book

This book is designed to provide relevant information quickly. The anecdotes illustrate the lessons in the bulleted tips that follow. Each section is a stand-alone lesson so that you can go directly to the information that you need for your particular situation. Some points appear in more than one chapter. Not surprisingly, those lessons are particularly important. I would appreciate feedback at www.swimminglessonsforbabysharks.com.

Preface

"I would much prefer to be a judge than a coal miner because of the absence of falling coal."—Peter Cook

Congratulations. You have chosen a fascinating and challenging profession. Learning to practice law can also seem daunting. But if you can make it through law school, you can learn how to apply the skills you attained to the actual practice of law. Your learning does not end with the bar exam, and you will make mistakes as you learn to practice law. Although this book contains anecdotes about lots of mistakes that new lawyers have made, the point is to help keep *you* from making them.

While perfection is an admirable goal, you don't have to attain it to stay employed and even thrive. One new associate commented that he committed five of my top-ten goofs in his first year of practice. Although the mistakes were painful and he wished he had avoided them, he is still employed at one of the nation's largest law firms and is doing well.

Your employer has a lot invested in you and will give you the benefit of the doubt—as long as it appears that you care and will be able to execute on the technical skills that are necessary to succeed. One thing that most irks senior lawyers is new lawyers who do not seem to take their jobs seriously. Although a primary focus of the book is succeeding in private practice, most of the practice tips should be useful in any practice setting.

A huge part of any successful law practice is being diligent—perhaps more diligent than you have ever been in your life. A healthy dose of paranoia will serve you well. Check, double-check, and triple-check. And regularly think about ways you can be more helpful.

Practicing law can be challenging, and you are likely to have to work long hours. Use that time to develop skills that will expand your opportunities. The job can be incredibly invigorating, as well. Few professions provide as much intellectual stimulation, and the rush from successfully completing a major transaction or winning a lawsuit can be amazing.

It is a luxury to work with smart, dedicated people in a profession where you can make a difference. The perks are not bad either. Being a lawyer has many advantages, not the least of which is a noticeable absence of falling coal.

Good luck. And focus, focus, focus.

Introduction

There is an occasional segment on *The Late Show with David Letterman* called: "Will It Float?" As the name suggests, the skit involves tossing an unusual object into a pool of water to see whether it sinks or floats. The participants engage in extensive speculation about the fate of the object before the toss. Then, with great fanfare, the object is hurled into the water. Often, the object sinks. The parallels to new lawyers arriving on the scene at their first jobs are inescapable.

Practically from day one, associates are expected to start practicing law and billing large amounts of money to clients. The problem is that no one has taught associates how to practice law. Law school is about academia—not the nuts and bolts of day-to-day practice.

With few opportunities in law school to learn about the actual practice of law and with little time at firms for training, it is no wonder that only a handful of new lawyers ever become partners at their firms. The vast majority decide to leave—or are asked to leave—long before being considered for partnership. The separation process is almost always painful and expensive for all involved.

In most cases, more training would have made the situation easier for both sides. Time and again, new lawyers leave one firm—only to succeed at their third or fourth employer. They finally "get it"—unfortunately, not before their third round of interviews, resumes, and uncomfortable goodbyes.

The cost of the revolving door is staggering. With most new associates making six-figure incomes from day one, new lawyers may have to stay at their firms at least a year just to break even. The amount of time lawyers spend recruiting and training replacements is time that can't be billed—and at a law firm, that's money down the drain.

The road from law school to law practice is particularly rough for new lawyers who have never worked another job. As smart as they may be, those new lawyers have to learn not only how to practice law, but also how to work in a business environment. Things like managing a calendar, getting to work on time every day, and producing documents without any typos may be second nature for anyone who has held a professional job. For someone coming to a firm directly out of school, even these basics can be a challenge.

At law firms in particular, there is no such thing as the "college try"—there is no "A" for effort. Grappling with the basics of work and how to practice law is often too much, causing many to flail for the first few years. The "failure rate" for new lawyers who never worked before law school is so high that many firms have an informal policy against hiring any new lawyers who have not held a professional job before law school.

Revenue pressures also constrain the amount of training that occurs. With partners' compensation tied closely to the revenue they generate, there is often a disincentive for partners to train associates because training often cannot be billed. Particularly if an associate does not appear to be a "quick study," it is often easier for lawyers to request help from another associate at the firm rather than mentor one who is struggling. This "sink or swim" nature is exacerbated by client efforts to reduce legal costs.

Associates have to have training to be valuable to the firm, but the more training that an associate needs, the more costly that associate is to the firm. That means associates have to learn very quickly. If an associate requires too much supervision, senior lawyers will take the path of least resistance and bypass that associate when giving out work. The associate's work dries up, it becomes impossible to meet the firm's billable-hour requirements, and the associate is asked to leave. Known as the "death spiral" at many firms, this process can happen alarmingly quickly. Law firms are not nurturing places.

This book includes practical advice from lawyers around the country. The goal is simple: to help associates succeed. New associates fail for many reasons. And just as good driving skills do not prevent car crashes, practical lawyering skills will not create bliss and fulfillment for every new lawyer. Still, better lawyering skills should help reduce the associate fatality rate.

Table of Contents

CHAPTER 1

SINK OR SWIM: THE TRANSITION FROM LAW SCHOOL TO LAW PRACTICE

YOUR CHOICE FOR THE SUMMER: FRISBEE OR TEST PREP?

You can lay the foundation for success at your first job before you ever walk in the door. One of the most important ways is to pass the bar exam the first time. Consider your choice for the summer:

It's a warm, sunny day. Your friends are outside playing with their Frisbee-brand flying disk. You are inside—sullen—preparing for the bar exam. The moment of truth arrives: You get a text message; your friends want you to join them.

Stop and think. This is a good time to remind yourself that you need to do your very best to pass the bar exam—the first time.

Failing the bar puts you at a serious disadvantage right from the start. First, there are the perception problems. The news will travel throughout the firm, scattering seeds of doubt about your abilities. Other lawyers will wonder, "Did we make a hiring mistake? Why did he fail the bar exam?"

In addition to affecting the perception of other lawyers, failing the bar exam is likely to take a toll on your own psyche. Lawyers who are confident inspire confidence in other lawyers and clients. The opposite is also true. Failing the bar exam almost always erodes the confidence of new lawyers. Particularly as the time approaches for the results of your second exam, anxiety increases. Fail the bar twice,

1

and you will probably be fired. Unfortunately, worrying causes a lot of unnecessary pressure and misspent energy. This is time you could spend learning how to practice law and acclimating to the firm. With the need to focus on retaking the bar exam, you are likely to lag behind your peers in billable hours, creating the potential for further demerits.

Failing the bar also limits the work you can do until you become a licensed attorney. Since most brand-new lawyers do not work independently or sign pleadings, the issue might never arise. But if a lawyer on the fly needs you to sign a pleading, you can't help. And next time, that lawyer is likely to ask someone else.

Failing the bar exam may also put a damper on celebrations at work. The firm will want to celebrate the success of those who passed—but won't want to hurt the feelings of anyone who didn't. So the bar-passing party might be postponed for six months—or might be more low-key than usual. All of that is uncomfortable. It is far better to pass with everyone else.

Bar Review Study Tips

Here are some tips for your bar exam preparation:

- ☐ Take your bar exam preparation very seriously; don't short yourself on study time—no matter what.

- ☐ Take a bar review class.

- ☐ Take practice tests or do whatever else you need to overcome test anxiety.

- ☐ Make sure your surroundings are comfortable in the days before and during the exam.

- ☐ At the exam, limit your interaction with fellow test-takers—particularly the anxious ones. Little good can come from conversing with other test-takers. If you talk to someone who appears cool and collected, you may well feel inadequate; if you talk to panicky participants, you may well absorb their anxiety.

NO "A" FOR EFFORT

As you begin your practice, it is important to understand some fundamental differences between learning the law in law school and the actual practice of law.

"There is no 'A for effort,'" a partner groused about an associate who'd spent lots of time researching a legal question without coming up with an answer.

That statement encapsulates many of the differences between the "real world" and law school. For new lawyers who had another career before law school, those differences may be more obvious. But if you come straight from school, the transition can be particularly challenging: You have to learn not only how to practice law, but also how to thrive in a business environment.

One of the most fundamental differences between legal practice and law school is that your work affects others. And the stakes are often high. Clients may stand to gain or lose significant rights (or a bundle of money) as a result of your legal work.

Not surprisingly, clients want results, and telling a client you can't find an answer isn't an option. There is also no "partial credit" for a partly right answer. In practice, an answer that isn't completely right is simply not the right answer. It's as if in law school there were only two grades: A's and F's.

As a student, you excel or flounder on your own. But at a firm, you are part of an organization and your work affects others in the firm, particularly the partners. Law firms have reputations—often carefully tended over generations. Your actions reflect on the firm, and an embarrassing moment for one lawyer in the firm can be an embarrassment for all.

Consider the following story: A new lawyer was making some calls to gather information on a legal issue. One of those calls was to the client. Somehow, the new lawyer did not realize he was talking with the client. This became apparent to the client at an awkward point in the conversation. Not surprisingly, the client got upset and called his regular lawyer at the firm to complain about the "idiot" associate who did not even know that he was talking to his own client.

Inane actions are bad enough because firms pride themselves on appearing smart—that's one of the main reasons people pay big bucks to law firms. But bigger screw-ups can subject the firm to legal liability. An error in law school will get you a low grade; an error at a firm can cost the other lawyers a lot of money. Malpractice insurance premiums are a huge part of a firm's costs, and deductibles are often in the six figures. Worse still, the bad publicity surrounding a malpractice claim could cost the firm more than an adverse judgment. As a new lawyer, you must be careful.

As a participant in a business enterprise, you also have to keep in mind that when you prepare a memo for a client, you are in many ways selling a product. The memo cannot be the purely academic exercise it was in law school. The work has to be useful, look good, be produced in a reasonable amount of time, and cost an amount that the client is willing to pay. In law school, if you wanted to, you could spend endless hours researching and writing an article. At a firm, the amount of time you spend has to bear some relation to the amount of money that the client is willing to pay. Otherwise, firms have to write off time. That means the firm paid you to do work that it gave the client for free. That is not a proposition any firm will continue for long.

The appearance and timeliness of your work are extremely important in the actual practice of law. Professors may overlook tardiness and typos in documents. Clients and supervising attorneys will not. A client may not necessarily know the difference between high-quality legal work and mediocre legal work (although senior lawyers will). A client will notice typos and is likely to assume that if your work has typos, the substance itself is shoddy. A client will also notice whether you met the deadline.

YOU ARE NOT A SUPERSTAR

One of the most important pieces of advice for brand-new lawyers is to keep your head down and work. The perks and praise associated with recruiting often come to an abrupt halt once associates join the firm. This can be a rude awakening for some associates. You may still be riding the high of graduation, securing a job, and all the perks that come with recruiting. But the firm has moved on. It is focused on recruiting the next year's lawyers and expects its new associates to get to work and learn.

The regular praise that is so much a part of the recruiting process may also dry up. And the fact that you may have graduated from a fancy law school with honors matters little once you join the firm. Suddenly, you know less than everyone else besides the other members of your class.

Because it takes time and effort to train new associates, some lawyers don't like to do it. They prefer to work with more senior associates—or do work themselves. Ask these lawyers for work, and you are likely to be turned down, politely or otherwise.

All of this can make for a difficult transition for associates who are used to being treated like superstars. Once you are hired, you will be expected to work hard—without complaint. When I asked one attorney to tell me the most important advice he would give new associates, he immediately said: "No whining."

Practicing law is demanding. It can be a grind. But if the job were easy, you would not be paid at least four times the salary of a barista at Starbucks. To a great extent, everyone at a law firm must justify their existence every single day. As a new lawyer, you have to earn the trust of more senior lawyers before you will get a steady stream of work or be allowed to interact with clients.

On the Bottom of the Heap

These reminders will go a long way toward easing your transition from law school star to new lawyer:

- ☐ Check your ego at the door—and be ready to learn.
- ☐ Be friendly and respectful to colleagues and staff members.
- ☐ Do *any* work you are given—and make it as perfect as possible.

☐ Don't take it personally if lawyers won't give you work. Just be persistent—and don't hesitate to ask less senior lawyers for work.

☐ Ask for feedback and accept it graciously.

☐ Don't complain or try to change the firm.

FIRST IMPRESSIONS MATTER

I was at lunch at the end of my stint as a summer associate. The partner looked at me sternly and said, "Your first six months at the firm are very important. You have to make a good first impression." It was the best career advice I ever received.

Law firms do their best to staff leanly. When you walk in the door, there will be lawyers who desperately need help with work for their clients. You have the potential to make the lives of those lawyers easier or more difficult. If you find useful information in a reasonable amount of time, their lives are easier. If you screw up, their lives are more difficult. Word spreads about mistakes, and if other lawyers don't trust your work, the work will stop coming. Unfortunately, it can take a long time to build a good reputation, but a bad one can form quickly.

A Good Impression

Here are some tips for making a good impression:

☐ Remember that other lawyers are your clients and that there are few second chances at law firms.

☐ Try to anticipate other lawyers' needs.

☐ Work hard.

☐ Show enthusiasm for the firm and your work.

☐ Take ownership of your work.

☐ Don't treat projects for associates as less important than projects for more senior lawyers.

☐ Be responsive and check in regularly with the assigning lawyer.

☐ Double-check everything.

☐ With the help of your assistant (if you have one) or other staff, make sure your documents are formatted correctly and have no typos.

☐ Refrain from using your mobile device while talking to colleagues or clients. They expect and deserve your full attention.

☐ Dress at least as professionally as the senior lawyers in your practice area.

☐ Be punctual.

UNDERSTANDING YOUR REAL JOB

As a new associate, you will be asked to do many things. Regardless of the particular tasks involved, you need to stay focused on accomplishing three goals in your first year.

1. Meet or exceed the firm's billable hour requirements.

2. Develop skills that are important to the firm.

3. Build relationships with one or two key lawyers by making their lives easier.

Making a good first impression will help with all three of these. If you do good work, you will get not only more work, but also more complex and challenging work that will help you learn and develop your skills.

Your value to the firm increases as you gain expertise and skills that are important to the firm. That's why you should take advantage of Continuing Legal Education, training for legal research services such as Westlaw, legal writing seminars, and other ways to increase your skills. With the pressure to bill, you may be tempted to give non-billable training short shrift. That's a mistake. Gaining expertise in an area that is important to the firm will enable you to get more interesting work. To be successful over the long term, you have to be more than a warm body.

Finally, you need to find one or two key partners at the firm who will invest in your success. At a law firm, the best way to stay employed and thrive is for a senior partner to tell her colleagues: "Without this associate to help with my work, I could not go out and get new business."

One new associate succinctly summarized the primary pathways to success at law firms:

> If you are a billing superstar, you may get a bonus. Having a powerful partner advocate for you is another way to get a bonus. That bonus is as much for the partner as the associate.

To become indispensable to a senior lawyer, you need to do useful, error-free work with minimal hand-holding. And that is what much of the rest of this book is about.

CHAPTER 2

HOW WELL DO YOU SWIM: YOUR FIRST EVALUATION

YOUR FIRST MAJOR TEST

Before you actually do much work, it helps to know how your work will be evaluated. Your first formal evaluation will probably come about six months after you start your job. If you don't receive a copy of your firm's evaluation form during your orientation—ask. It is always easier to do well on a test if you know the questions.

Those first six months on the job are critical because lawyers will form impressions about your work in a very short time. Just a few negative impressions may be tough to overcome.

Typically, firms run a report of all the hours you have recorded and then contact the attorneys responsible for those projects in order to get feedback about your performance. The firm may also talk with you in advance of the process. This is a good time to bring up any untoward incidents that may have arisen with another attorney.

New associates sometimes question whether they should bring up negative experiences early in the review process—or just respond if they come up during the review. Since it is highly unlikely that a negative incident will slip through the cracks, it is usually best to come clean as early as possible in the review process. This gives you a chance to explain the situation from your perspective—and most important, to show that you learned from the process. Certainly, the perspective about that incident that matters most is the partner's perspective—but if you demonstrate that you took responsibility and learned from the incident, it is not as likely to be held against you—as long as you do not repeat it.

Denying that there was a problem or blaming someone else—including the partner—will be frowned upon. You need to explain what happened from your point of view—especially what you did to resolve the problem and how you will make sure the problem does not recur.

One thing that you may have learned is that you came across a lawyer who is difficult to work for, but giving that as the reason for the problem is not a pathway to success. Just try to avoid that lawyer in the future. If you have to work for the lawyer, ask for pointers from other attorneys who work well with the difficult lawyer.

Lawyers will be asked to evaluate you based on several criteria, but they typically fall within four general categories: the quality of your work, the quantity of your work, the way you manage your work, and other lawyers' perceptions of your ability to generate new work in the future. A typical evaluation usually consists of rating associates with respect to whether they meet or exceed expectations or need improvement in the following key aspects of practicing law:

☐ **Quality of Work**

- ○ Legal knowledge
- ○ Analysis
- ○ Legal research
- ○ Drafting
- ○ Oral communication
- ○ Attention to detail
- ○ Creativity/problem solving
- ○ Appearance of work

☐ **Work Management**

- ○ Efficiency
- ○ Dependability
- ○ Educability

- ○   Independence
- ○   Ability to manage others
- ○   Advises on progress of matters
- ○   Organizational skills

☐ **Attitude and Judgment**

- ○   Initiative
- ○   Acceptance of criticism
- ○   Judgment
- ○   Interpersonal skills
- ○   Teamwork
- ○   Ethics

☐ **Client Relations**

- ○   Ability to inspire confidence
- ○   Ability to maintain clients

☐ **Contribution to Firm or Practice Group Administration**

- ○   Non-billable work, such as writing articles for the firm's bulletins or blogs
- ○   Firm committees
- ○   Pro-bono work

☐ **Economic Contribution**

- ○   Billable hours
- ○   Client development
- ○   Practice development

☐ **Poise**

- ○   Crisis management

WHAT THE "TEST" MEANS

Here is a breakdown of what those scoring criteria mean in real life:

Quality of Work

Legal knowledge. The firm expects you to gain legal knowledge in an area in which the firm currently makes money—or believes it can make money in the future.

Analysis. Analysis often trips up new associates because real life is not as tidy as most law school exams. It's easy to get lost in a morass of irrelevant facts. You'll get better with analysis over time, but two habits will give you a solid head-start. First, come up with a clear and concise statement of the law. (If you are dealing with a specific case, concisely state the holding.) Second, sort out the facts most critical to a particular result and go from there.

Legal research. Get as much training in legal research as possible. It's readily abundant at most firms, and excellent research skills are a great way to stand out early.

Drafting. Clear, concise writing is another good way to make your mark. Take a legal writing seminar or two.

Oral communication. You need to be able to explain and defend your work to the assigning lawyer clearly and confidently.

Attention to detail. This is critical. Double-check your work for big errors and little ones. Be particularly careful about facts and figures when it will be obvious whether you are right or wrong—such as dates. Have someone fastidious review your documents for typos, and always read the final version yourself, in its entirety, before turning it in to the assigning lawyer.

Creativity/problem solving. This means you use your brain to help achieve the client's goals.

Appearance of work. With everything else you have to do, this may seem like putting form over substance, but legal work is expensive; your documents need to look professional.

Work Management

Efficiency. To be efficient, you have to know how much time the senior lawyer thinks a project should take—or stated another way, how much it is worth to the client. Always ask at the beginning of a project.

Dependability. "Dropping the ball" is one of the most dreaded phrases in the practice of law. Don't do it. Use electronic gadgets, a pad of paper, rubber bands around your wrist—whatever, but don't forget to do what you have agreed to do. You won't get any slack for forgetting a task.

Educability. Ask for feedback, make sure you understand it, and follow it.

Independence. This one is tricky for a new associate. You need to check in regularly with senior lawyers to make sure that you aren't spinning your wheels. You also need to use your brain and add value to a project. Greater independence will come with time. Early on, err on the side of checking in, but gather your thoughts in advance to show that you respect the senior lawyer's time.

Ability to manage others. This is not critical for brand-new lawyers. Just get along with paralegals and other assistants.

Advises on progress of matters. Don't leave people guessing about your progress on a project.

Organizational skills. If another lawyer has given you a document and then asks for that document, you need to be able to find it immediately.

Attitude and Judgment

Initiative. This happens when you go into a lawyer's office and say, "What else can I do to help?" Or you anticipate what may be needed on the case and ask if it would be helpful. Don't just go off and do projects on your own, though. That's called doing work that may not be billed.

Acceptance of criticism. Practicing law is not easy. If you get criticism, view it as an opportunity to learn. Just don't make the same mistake twice.

Judgment. Judgment is akin to common sense. Exercising good judgment is simply being aware of the consequences of potential courses of action and taking the course of action that will come closest to achieving the desired result. There are a zillion ways to exercise bad judgment but, fortunately, one way to help prevent it: Stop and think.

Interpersonal skills. Law firms can be pressure cookers: Be congenial and helpful, but not a door-mat, and *always* keep it together.

Teamwork. This means you willingly pitch in even if it requires some personal sacrifices.

Client relations. At the outset, your clients are other lawyers at the firm. If you gain their confidence, they will eventually trust you to interact with clients. But don't push it. Gaining expertise in the law and learning the client's business need to come first.

Ethics. It's your career that's at stake: Do the right thing.

Contribution to Firm or Practice Group Administration

There are always ample opportunities to do administrative work at a firm—and too much non-billable work is detrimental to your career. You should be strategic about your non-billable work. Writing articles for the firm blog is far better than serving on the holiday party committee.

Economic Contribution

Doing quality work is the best way to keep getting enough work to meet your billable-hour requirements. Find out whether it is acceptable at your firm to meet the stated requirements—or whether there is an unwritten rule that you must exceed them. In any event, you need to be billing about as many hours as the other associates in your class. Keep in mind that if you exceed your firm's billable-hour standards in your first year, the firm is likely to expect you to bill at least the same number of hours the following year.

Poise

You need to maintain a professional appearance and demeanor. Keep it together, particularly in a crisis.

Often your job as a lawyer is to turn chaos into serenity. No meltdowns allowed.

JUST ONE RULE: NEVER SCREW UP

A lawyer in the Midwest once joked that working at his firm was easy because there was only one rule: Never screw up. He was only partly kidding.

Clients typically view lawyers as a necessary evil—necessary because the client's problem is serious and the client has not been able to solve it alone. Evil, because litigation in particular is so expensive and distracting for companies that they usually try to avoid it at all costs. By the time a matter ends up at a law firm, it is often a mess and there is no more room for error.

Practicing law is difficult, but with some care, you can avoid the mistakes that frequently get new lawyers in trouble. While many of these seem obvious, unfortunately, they happen time and again.

Top 10 Goofs to Avoid

Your life as a lawyer will be easier if you avoid these goofs:

1. Blowing a deadline or forgetting a task

2. Citing an overruled case or repealed statute in a legal document

3. Coming up with the wrong answer to a legal question that has a fairly definite answer

4. Not finding the answer to a legal question that has a fairly definite answer

5. Revealing confidential information

6. Contradicting another lawyer in front of a client

7. Failing to track all of your time

8. Trying to cover up a mistake

9. Failing to proofread documents

10. Flipping attitude to other lawyers or staff

DEALING WITH THE GOOFS YOU DON'T AVOID

Most of these goofs can be avoided by paying attention to details and double-checking your work. A huge part of being a good lawyer is being reliable—that is, coming up with the right answer to legal problems on time. That means you check your work for accuracy and don't cite legal precedents that have been overruled. You don't miss deadlines. You check—and double-check—due dates and meet them. You also don't forget small tasks such as returning phone calls.

Your research must be thorough and creative so that you find a useful answer to the client's problem. When the senior lawyer searches for an answer, she should not come up with anything better than you did. And do not ever give short shrift to proofing documents.

Another big goof involves trimming your time records. The constant admonition at law firms is to track all of your time. But there is always some tension between being careful and being efficient. On occasion, new lawyers wonder whether they should underreport their time to avoid appearing inefficient. That's a Hobson's choice, but one easily resolved: It is better to seem inefficient than lazy. Track all of your time.

The remaining goofs in the Top 10 list deal with people skills. While it's sometimes okay to show some bravado with opposing counsel—that can be a necessary part of your job—with coworkers, keep your ego in check. Your colleagues will not appreciate your being a jerk in the office. Law firms are stressful enough without an excessive number of prima donnas and jerks erupting at random. Young jerks are especially frowned upon. Getting along with colleagues and staff is also a good way to show the firm that you can build positive relationships with clients. (And it's very helpful when you find out that you need 5,000 copies of a document in fifteen minutes.)

You will not be perfect, so when you realize you have made a mistake, 'fess up as soon as possible. Failing to do so will be perceived as a sign of weakness and will only make things worse. The more time that passes between your mistake and the time you disclose it and start working to correct it, the bigger the problem. It is almost as if there is a clock that starts ticking as soon as you screw up; the sooner you turn it off by reporting the problem, the better off you are.

Take comfort in the fact that it is unlikely a beginning attorney could figure out how to make an entirely new type of error, so most likely it's been done before and is relatively easy to fix if addressed promptly. If you wait, the mistake might not be as easy to fix. And it will not just go away.

It's far better to catch your own mistakes than to have someone else catch them. When you report a problem, it is best to be able to suggest a solution to that problem—as long as coming up with a solution does not significantly delay your coming clean. If a lot of time passes between the time you make an error and the time you discover and begin to resolve it, you are likely to look like either a slacker or a dissembler.

Lawyers must be able to trust your work, so if you do make a mistake, take the course of action most likely to maintain trust. It may be okay to fix some small errors without falling on your sword. But if someone is likely to find out about a mistake, be sure that person hears about it from you first.

That said, there is no need to make a fetish about apologizing or to tell all your colleagues about your mistake. That may just lead to unhelpful gossip. Tell the people who need to know and move on.

CUTTING THROUGH THE CURRENTS WITH EASE: 10 QUICK TIPS

Lawyers are busy, so here is a quick list of ten things you can do to help ensure your success as a new lawyer:

1. **Make a good first impression.** A misstep early is much more harmful than one later on.

2. **Meet your billable-hour targets.**

3. **Find a mentor—or two.** Ask younger lawyers who appear to be doing well to give you advice.

4. **Resist attempting to change the firm.** New lawyers inevitably see things that they would change. At first, it's best just to keep your head down and work.

5. **Befriend support staff.** Support staff can be incredibly helpful; get them on your side.

6. **Take responsibility.** Anything that smacks of "I don't care" drives senior lawyers crazy.

7. **Be ready to learn.** No one who has just graduated from law school is very adept at practicing law. Take advantage of every opportunity to learn.

8. **Ask for feedback.** Feedback is one of the best ways to learn, and you may not get it if you do not ask.

9. **Find one thing that you can do better than almost anyone, and let others know.** Your skill may be finding cases online that elude everyone else. Whatever it is, if you can become the "go-to" attorney for something the firm needs, you will be way ahead of the game.

10. **Take a writing seminar.** The legal research and writing class in law school is the bane of most students' existence. However, for practicing law, it is probably one of the most important classes in law school. Writing clearly, concisely, and persuasively is critical to your success.

CHAPTER 3

FEEDING WITH FELLOW SHARKS: GETTING AND DOING WORK

DAY THREE: WHAT TO EXPECT

It's day three. You are sitting at your desk. Your orientation is over and you have ordered office supplies. Other lawyers have mentioned that you will be working on a "big case" that just came into the firm. The senior partner involved is going to talk to you about it, but she is at a seminar.

In other words, at that moment, sitting at your desk, you have absolutely nothing to do. You can arrange your pencils, order more office supplies, or look out the window, but until you talk to the senior partner, you have no billable work—and instinctively you know this is not a good thing.

Some new lawyers will arrive at a firm to find that they are completely inundated with work from the start. But for most new lawyers, it takes a while to get a reliable stream of work. Sitting at my desk on the third day, I realized that working at a law firm was much different from most jobs. I expected to bill hours. That was a given. What I did not expect was to have to drum up my own work—particularly right from the start.

The work allocation process at most firms can be described charitably as "flexible" or, less charitably, as "haphazard." Typically, at least one senior lawyer is responsible for involving you in projects and trying to get other lawyers to do the same. Firms also use a variety of other methods to ensure that new lawyers have meaningful work. But regard-

19

less of the variations in the work-allocation processes, one rule holds true: Even as a new lawyer at a firm, you are ultimately responsible for making sure that you have enough billable work. In other words, right from the start, you are basically self-employed, and you are responsible for managing and building your practice.

In some ways, you are like a highly paid taxi driver. The firm gives you the tools to do your job and shows you the ropes. But you have to find work yourself—first from other lawyers and then from clients. Don't forget that first step. In the beginning, other lawyers are your *clients*, and you have to do good work so they want to give you more.

When I first started at a firm, the notion of having to drum up my own work and also being responsible for meeting a billable-hour quota seemed patently unfair. I thought, "How could I be responsible for failing to meet an hours quota if no one gave me work?" One answer is "Welcome to the real world." A better answer is that one of your primary responsibilities as a new lawyer is to develop relationships with other lawyers who will give you enough work to keep you busy.

Getting work may take some persistence at first. When you are starting out, most lawyers will be able to do work in less time than it will take to teach you how to do the project. Training takes time, and lawyers who do it are making an investment in you. The investment is usually non-billable for the senior lawyers and typically doesn't pay off for quite some time. That can mean you have to knock on several doors to ask for new projects when you see your workload dwindling. The process can be uncomfortable, particularly when other lawyers seem too busy to come up with projects or politely give you the brush-off. If you show promise, though, most lawyers will take the time to work with you because they know that in the long run, you can make their lives easier. The unwritten compact is: "You make my life easier; I will help give you enough work to keep you employed."

You Eat What You Kill: Getting Work

Here are a few important reminders about getting work:

- [ ] You are primarily responsible for getting enough work to meet or exceed the billable-hour requirements and for managing and building your own practice.

- [ ] Your mentor or practice group leader can help you find billable work—if you ask.

- [ ] Read conflicts reports every day to see what new matters have come into the firm. If a case seems interesting, contact the lawyer listed and ask to work on the project.

- [ ] Start asking for work before you need it because it may take a few days for lawyers to come up with projects.

- [ ] Lawyers' initial requests may seem unreasonable, but those requests are often negotiable; the assigning attorneys probably have no idea how much other work you have.

- [ ] Some people may not have your best interests in mind. If this turns out to be the case, try to get work from other lawyers. One new lawyer found that his associate mentor just gave him nonbillable work that his mentor did not want to do: "His ostensible role was to help me get billable work. That never happened."

KNOCKING ON DOORS:
HOW TO ASK FOR WORK

When you need to get out and drum up work, there are a few items to consider before you leave your office:

- [ ] **Do your homework.** Early on, find out about the work styles and reputation of other lawyers in the firm. If a senior lawyer gives *all* associates poor reviews or has a reputation for being completely disorganized, you may not want to open that door.

☐ **Ask your mentor.** Most firms assign a lawyer to each new associate to help make sure the new lawyer stays busy. Some firms have a policy that all work for a particular associate is to be funneled through the mentoring attorney. At many firms, this rarely happens. In any event, start by talking with the attorney who is supposed to make sure you stay busy—or with other attorneys in your practice area.

☐ **Start with your own group.** Large firms may want you to specialize as quickly as possible, so you may be expected to start looking for work in your own practice area. Other practice groups may not be as receptive to your inquiries about work because they probably have their own associates to keep busy. And if you are not going to be working in a particular area of the law over the long term, those lawyers will be reluctant to invest their time in training you.

☐ **Cast your net farther.** Just because you should start your search for work within your own practice group does not mean that you should limit yourself to your own practice group if you are not coming up with anything. You need to stay busy. Likewise, if a lawyer from another practice group approaches you about a project, agree to do it if you have time. But before definitely committing to work for another practice group, check with your own practice group. And of course, work for your practice group should usually get first priority.

☐ **Show commitment.** It is helpful to show a commitment to a particular area of the law. Straddling two practice areas can be a challenge. As one attorney put it, "You only get half the love, and the two departments don't know if you love them at all."

☐ **Finish first.** It is bad form to ask for work from a lawyer when you have a project for that lawyer that you have not completed—unless you are very close to having the project completed.

☐ **Know your schedule.** Before you ask for work, figure out how much time you can devote to new projects and within what timeframe. An inevitable question will be: "How much time do you have?" You should be able to answer it with some amount of accuracy. Lawyers will want to know when you can start—and finish—a project.

☐ **Give advance notice.** Don't wait until you are completely out of projects to ask for new ones. It will take time for other lawyers to come up with projects. You may want to say, "In a few days, I will have some time, if you have some upcoming projects."

☐ **Do stellar work.** The best way to get regular work without having to go begging is to do superior work for a lawyer who is willing to invest time in helping you learn.

☐ **Stagger your requests.** If you do good work, lots of lawyers will want you to help out. If you have asked several lawyers for work and the next day they all come up with projects, you can't tell half of them, "Sorry, I have enough work now."

☐ **Don't be too picky.** When you cast your net, you may snag some projects that aren't particularly palatable. Until you establish yourself, you should rarely refuse them. When you ask some lawyers for work, they may be all too willing to unload their non-billable projects on you. That, of course, is not what you meant when you asked for work, but by asking for work, you have made it clear that you have time to take on projects.

☐ **Make your needs known.** To avoid getting too much non-billable work, you can start your inquiries along the lines of "I need to keep up my hours, so I am wondering if you have any billable work that I could help with." This way, the lawyer will have a somewhat harder time suggesting non-billable work because the lawyer will already know that will not meet your needs.

☐ **Use judgment.** If you are trying to build a relationship with a particular lawyer, you should do any work that lawyer asks. But if the lawyer wants you to do a huge amount of non-billable work and very little billable work, you should think about supporting lawyers who are more balanced with their work allocation.

☐ **Remember: Any work is better than no work.** As the saying goes, "Beggars can't be choosers," but if you truly believe that taking on particular work will cause you more harm than good, you can (and should) say that another lawyer has also asked you about some projects and you just need to check to make sure about deadlines, time commitments, etc. That will give you time to gracefully figure out a way to get other billable work so that you in fact are "too busy" or to otherwise gracefully decline. Keep in mind, though, that if you have very little to do, you should not turn down any work—even non-billable work from Satan.

COMPLETING YOUR FIRST PROJECTS

Early on I learned that it is very difficult to complete an assignment that you do not understand. The partner was in a rush when he gave me the assignment. The subject was also complex, and I did not want to appear dense. So I just nodded—even though I didn't understand much of what he said. There was a letter from the client and some preliminary research materials, so I decided it would be better to figure it out myself rather than to appear slow. I took the papers back to my desk and read them. When I was finished, I still had no idea what I was supposed to do. After a few minutes of stewing, I tracked down the attorney and said I needed to "clarify" the assignment—in other words, "Please start over from the top." This time, I sucked up my pride and asked questions and then confirmed exactly what I was supposed to do. All of that made starting the project much easier.

When you first get a project from another attorney, you need to find out at least five things:

1. The specific client or clients that you represent (This is not always obvious if affiliated entities are involved.)

2. The exact problem that you are being asked to solve

3. How much time the attorney thinks you should spend on the project

4.   How the attorney wants you to provide the information (memo, oral discussion, etc.)

5.   When the attorney wants your work

New associates are often reticent about asking questions when they get an assignment. But the need for clarity does not simply evaporate. If you don't know exactly what you are supposed to do, it is unlikely that you will just happen to complete a project correctly—and certainly not without spinning your wheels.

When you start practicing law, there is a huge amount to learn. You may not be familiar with specialized legal terms, acronyms, or obscure aspects of a client's business. Take the initiative to look up things that you can find out yourself. Otherwise, ask. Other lawyers who are deeply involved in a matter may assume that they have given you information when in fact they haven't. Even if you think you understand the assignment precisely, get in the habit of repeating your understanding so that the assigning attorney can correct or modify the assignment. You will almost always get more useful information that way.

Sometimes you may not understand an assignment because the assigning attorney has not thought it through carefully. Your questions will ultimately end up saving both of you time. Once you understand the exact assignment, write it down.

Throughout the project, lean toward "over-communicating" to make sure you are on track. Getting halfway into a project only to realize you are not sure what the assigning lawyer expects you to be doing is frustrating for not only you, but also the senior lawyer. Having to ask questions at that late point means tracking down the lawyer who gave you the project immediately to ask questions that will probably indicate you have spent fruitless time on an assignment.

When you first get an assignment, ask whether there is other information that would be helpful for you to know to complete the project. For example, it's usually helpful to find out how your work relates to other legal work that the lawyer is doing for the client.

Because lawyers are busy, you should assume that you have only one chance to find out everything you need to know before you have to complete the assignment. In many cases, that is close to the truth. With lawyers in meetings and traveling hither and yon, you may not be able to talk to the lawyer more than once in person—if at all. However, as soon as you realize you have a question about what you should be doing, try to contact the lawyer—in person, by e-mail, or by phone—so that you don't spin your wheels as the deadline ticks away. If you don't complete the project correctly by the deadline, the fact that you could not get information from the attorney involved won't be any excuse.

Knowing how much time the attorney expects you to spend on the project is vital because it often reflects the senior attorney's estimate of how much the project is worth to the client. If you spend $50,000 worth of time coming up with an answer that will save a client $20,000, you haven't done the client any favors. The lawyer's estimate of the amount of time is just that—an estimate. The assigning lawyer can't know exactly what will be involved in solving a particular problem, and you can't stop working unless you have come up with an acceptable answer. In any event, you should check in when you have spent close to the amount of time that the lawyer expected the project to take. And you should never cut corners in order to be "efficient." Coming up with the wrong answer in ten hours is far worse than coming up with the right answer in fifteen hours.

Find out exactly the kind of work product the attorney expects, but keep in mind that the attorney may want you to discuss your answer before deciding whether a written product is necessary. If your answer makes sense and will be useful to the client, you will probably be asked to put it in writing. If not, the lawyer is unlikely to want to waste the client's money by putting the information into a memo.

Finally, be sure you know the assigning lawyer's deadline—and then plan to complete the project *before* the deadline. You may get sidetracked on other projects—so never put off a project until the last minute. Meeting the deadline is critical because clients often cannot make important decisions until they receive advice from their lawyers. Often, clients know what they want to do and simply need some assurance that their plans won't run afoul of the law. That means that when a client has asked a legal question, it is likely the client has put certain plans on hold while your firm addresses the legal issues. The sooner you can come up with an answer, the better—assuming it is correct.

Project Checklist

This checklist should help you stay on course in completing your projects.

☐ Learn the work style and idiosyncrasies of the lawyers who assigned the work; if possible read some samples of their letters or memos.

☐ Check in with the assigning lawyer regularly to make sure you understand the assignment and are making the progress she expects. (If you think you may be checking in too much or too little, just ask.)

☐ Find out how your work fits into the bigger picture.

☐ Let the assigning lawyer know if the project is taking significantly more time than expected— that is a sign that you are off track.

☐ Document what you did on the assignment, including all of the legal authorities you reviewed, so that senior lawyers can independently verify your work.

☐ Try to finish the assignment *before* the deadline.

☐ Proofread carefully.

☐ Ask another associate to look at your work and give you feedback before you turn it in to the assigning lawyer. (This may require you to buy your colleague drinks.)

☐ Do not give the assigning lawyer work that is a "draft." The assigning lawyer will not know whether your work is a mess because you have said it is a draft or because you just do substandard work. The lawyer will probably only remember that your work was a mess.

☐ When you finish the project, talk to the assigning lawyer about your work before turning it in. If it appears you missed the mark and there is time left before the deadline, you can make changes to the document to reflect your discussion.

CHAPTER 4

SWIMMING WITH SHARKS: BUILDING RELATIONSHIPS WITH OTHER LAWYERS

THE STACK OF PAPERS: HOW NOT TO ENDEAR YOURSELF TO OTHER LAWYERS

I once worked for a public relations firm that touted its goal of "being as indispensable to our clients as they are to us." A similar goal will serve you well with senior lawyers at your firm. At first, other lawyers will be your clients, and your main job is to do everything possible to make their lives easier. Unfortunately, that is often a challenge for new lawyers. My experience with the stack of papers is a case in point.

About six o'clock one evening, I was putting the finishing touches on a brief I'd been working on all day. (And which, of course, was due the next day.) I needed to fill in a blank with a case citation to support an argument in the brief—nothing dramatic or obscure, just a nice touch for emphasis, an exclamation point. An associate was tracking down the citation. We had talked about it a couple of days before, and though she had gotten behind, she assured me in our e-mail communications throughout the day that she was close. She said she would have something by the end of the day. Indeed she did.

Harried, she rushed into my office with a stack of papers. A *foot* high. I was puzzled since I needed "a" citation to support the argument. Pleadings have page limits, after all.

With some trepidation, I asked about the stack of papers. She said they were cases that I might want to look at. At 6 p.m., I did not want to look at *any* cases. I wanted to fill in the blank in my brief and go home. I reiterated that I needed only one or two cases. She replied that she could not decide which ones were best, so she brought them all—so I could decide. I asked if she had put them in any kind of order, for example, the ones she thought were the best.

"No," she said. She really could not decide which ones were the best, but she said she had highlighted portions of each case that she thought were most important. I was relieved, at least, that I would not have to wade through the entirety of a small law library's worth of cases at 6 p.m. the day before a brief was due—all to fill in a small blank to support a small argument.

But my relief was short-lived. As I flipped through the cases, I saw page after page after page highlighted in pink. Clearly more than one highlighter had been sacrificed to the cause, and I knew that just reading the pink portions would take me several hours.

A monkey can mark papers with a highlighter. But in this case, the highlighting did not look entirely indiscriminate. I knew some judgment had gone into the process, so I had a glimmer of hope that the associate could still help me narrow the field. I tried again by asking, "If you could pick just one or two of the cases to support the argument, which ones would they be?"

She couldn't say. "I think you should look at *all* of them," she said. And she added without missing a beat, "I also tabbed some other citations that you might want to look up yourself." Sure enough, there were about fifty sticky notes throughout the cases, with arrows pointing to citations of other cases. She said the tabbed cases looked interesting, and I might want to look those up and read them, as well. With that, she bolted for her bus and disappeared through the door.

With a sigh—and a vow to get even—I dove into the sea of pink. The cases were not in any discernible order: lower court, Supreme Court, new case, ancient case—all thrown together. I soon decided that it would be quicker for me to find a case myself than to try to sort through the mass of pink cases with yellow sticky notes. I went online and in about half an hour found a couple of cases that would suffice. It then dawned on me that the associate had probably spent at least two days— thousands of dollars of billable time—researching, reading, and highlighting to compile a stack of material that ended up being completely useless.

Earning Your Keep

Here are some important tips about earning your keep:

☐ **Get a handle on the assignment.** Be sure you understand the assignment and are doing *exactly* what was assigned. Doing more is not always better, but it is always more expensive.

☐ **Use your brain.** That sounds obvious, but new lawyers are often afraid to make decisions or reach conclusions. Still, that is what you are being paid to do. If other lawyers did not think you were capable of handling the particular project, they would not have assigned it. If you don't use your brain for fear that you will come up with the wrong answer, you demonstrate only that you couldn't handle the assignment. Remember: A monkey can highlight cases in pink. You need to exercise judgment.

☐ **Do your job.** Do not tell supervising lawyers to track down cases or check things that you could check yourself. Your job is to make other lawyers' jobs easier—not harder.

☐ **Organize and synthesize to add value.** Present information in a logical, organized way. Practicing law involves huge amounts of information that has to be organized and presented in a persuasive manner. Thus, organizing and synthesizing information is one of the most important functions you can provide as you are starting out. You should always present information in some logical order and do whatever else you can to make it easier to review the information, such as highlighting the date or the jurisdiction, or having your assistant put materials in notebooks. The approach you take will vary depending on the project and the supervising lawyer. But the bottom line is always the same: Make the information as useful as possible with as little effort on the part of the other lawyer as possible.

☐ **Anticipate needs.** Regularly think of ways to be helpful on projects and make those suggestions to the senior lawyers. If you suggest something to a partner and the partner dismisses it, go back and ask why your suggestion was rejected. You should include the reasons that you thought things should have been done one way. The partner may know that the client has a particular business need that makes your suggestion unworkable—or the partner simply may not have been paying attention and just gave a knee-jerk response. Whatever response you get, you will have learned something—and you will have demonstrated initiative and strategic thinking.

☐ **Be ready to help.** Being helpful sometimes requires preparation. For example, you should make sure you have a current passport if there is any chance you might need to travel outside the country. If you might need to go to court, keep appropriate clothes in your office in case you need to make a sudden appearance.

JUDGMENT DAY

Judgment is one of the most important qualities that senior lawyers look for in a new lawyer. It can also be one of the most elusive. Getting in the habit of always thinking before you act will serve you well. Impulsive behavior is not well-suited to the practice of law, and you don't want the reputation of being someone who shoots first and aims later.

Poor judgment comes in countless flavors. But asking yourself why you are doing something can help put the brakes on actions you may later regret. Although it is sometimes said that judgment can't be taught, people can almost always spot bad judgment in others. The discovery is usually accompanied by the refrain: "Can you believe that?"

If the Ivy League law school graduate had thought about it, she probably would not have passed around her high school cheerleading photo—which many people at the firm thought looked quite like a glamour shot.

Judgment is mostly a matter of considering the consequences of your actions—something you must do with respect to actions you take on behalf of your clients every day. The habit of thinking through the consequences of your actions needs to become second nature.

Considering consequences could have helped avoid these uncomfortable situations:

Hands-On Trouble. At a firm function one evening, several senior partners—all men—were sitting around a table drinking cocktails and playing poker. Many cocktails had been consumed by those playing poker—and others. At work functions, that is the first sign of danger. Various attorneys at the firm were milling about socializing and intermittently watching the game. A summer associate was among them. She believed it was important to get to know the partners better. What a good opportunity with several of them at the same table playing poker.

She started chatting them up and then began to dish out the compliments. Liquor flowed and inhibitions evaporated. Through the fog of alcohol, she did not realize that the lawyers mostly viewed her chatter as a distraction from their game. Since she was not getting the attention she thought she deserved, she upped the ante and brought up the fact that she had been a professional massage therapist before going to law school.

She began rubbing the shoulders of one of the partners at the table. Responding as one might after a few drinks, he said, "Uh, thanks." He did not vocalize the rest of the sentence, which was "and you just lost your job because I would much rather have sore shoulders than lose all my money in a sexual harassment lawsuit." Emboldened by the partner's apparent approval, she continued to practice her trade on others at the table. Onlookers were horrified.

At the end of the summer, everyone knew what was going to happen—except the associate. Her review came, and she was shocked to learn that she did not receive an offer of employment. The stated reason: "We just don't have enough business now in the areas in which you want to practice."

Lunch Largesse. The next example falls in the category of "too much of a good thing." Bob, a first-year associate, volunteered to serve as the annual "tour director" for summer associates to make sure they were meeting other lawyers and enjoying their summer. He took to the job with gusto. The firm had a policy of reimbursing lawyers for lunch—as long as they took along a summer associate. Bob was very social and greatly enjoyed the gravy train. He rounded up scads of summer associates and other lawyers for lunch practically every day. All the summer associates knew Bob, and many of them had been to lunch with him several times. In his first month as "tour director," Bob joked about how little of his own money he had spent on lunch.

When he turned in his receipts for reimbursement, the firm was not amused. In one month, he alone had spent more than the firm's entire budget for summer associate lunches. He hadn't thought to ask about a budget, and it never occurred to the firm that its largesse would be abused so badly. Bob's billable hours were also dismal because he had taken so many two-hour lunches. Firms care about the bottom line. You should too.

Think Before You Act

Asking yourself these questions before you act should save you some grief:

- ☐ How will this action advance my career?
- ☐ How will this action advance the goals of the firm—financial and otherwise?
- ☐ How will this help me gain the respect of other lawyers?
- ☐ How will this be perceived by others?
- ☐ Are other people doing what I am about to do?
- ☐ Is this necessary?
- ☐ Is this ethical?

And to avoid some of the most common landmines:

- ☐ Don't get intoxicated around your colleagues, period.
- ☐ Stay miles away from anything that smacks at all of sexual innuendo.

NOT SO FAST ... AVOIDING THE
PERILS OF E-MAIL

Urban legend has it that an executive at a large company sent out a routine e-mail to thousands of employees across the globe. One of them was the woman with whom he was having an affair. She was traveling overseas and missed him terribly. She promptly typed an e-mail response to tell him how she would express her passion when she returned. Then she realized to her horror that she had inadvertently sent a love missive to 15,000 colleagues. She returned to the country, but not to a job.

Whether or not that particular tale is true, many real-life horror stories abound. A parade of politicians and CEOs has been forced to resign when their e-mails revealed extramarital affairs. Michael Brown, former director of FEMA, looked like a sap when e-mails revealed that he joked about being a "fashion god" and was concerned about finding a dog sitter while Hurricane Katrina devastated New Orleans.

More recently, a newspaper obtained and printed steamy text messages from a big-city mayor to his lover (who was also an employee). The text messages were not only humiliating, but also contradicted their sworn testimony in an earlier lawsuit. Both lost their jobs and ended up with some solitary time to reflect on the whole snafu.

Despite near constant television exposés involving e-mail, clients need regular reminders to be circumspect in their e-mail communications. Lawyers need to be even more careful: At best, e-mail screw-ups erode a client's trust; at worst, they can constitute malpractice.

BEFORE YOU HIT "SEND"

E-mail is an incredibly useful tool for documenting your communications in writing, but there are many pitfalls. Here are some useful reminders:

☐ **Consider whether e-mail is the best mode of communication.** Communicating by e-mail can become almost automatic, which is the source of many e-mail embarrassments. You should think twice—or three times—before sending confidential, inflammatory, or personal

communications from your work e-mail. There
can also be confidentiality issues with e-mail.

☐ **Remember that personal interactions are
important.** Don't underestimate the benefits of
personal interactions with colleagues and clients. You need to get out of your office and meet
your colleagues in person. A face-to-face interaction communicates much more than is possible
with e-mail, including how you handle on-the-
spot questions and how you will present yourself
to clients. To fully assess your skills as a lawyer
and give appropriate guidance, your colleagues
need to talk with you in person. At least early in
your practice, make it a habit to respond to most
inquiries by going to the other lawyer's office.
Here's another tip: That lawyer is likely to be
busy when you arrive, so bring work to do while
you wait. Don't be stuck cooling your heels with
your meter off.

☐ **Be circumspect and professional.** In a large
organization, e-mails may be the only interactions you have with some lawyers—even if you
are diligent about face-to-face communications.
Make sure you know what kinds of internal
e-mails your firm allows. Some firms have set
up bulletin boards or special e-mail accounts for
solicitations, social gatherings, lost and found
items, and similar messages. When hundreds of
lawyers billing hundreds of dollars an hour open
and read unnecessary e-mails, thousands of dollars in time can be lost, and the lawyers will
remember who caused them to lose that time.
Concise, professional e-mails sent without typos
to the appropriate recipients demonstrate that
you are thoughtful and respect other lawyers'
time. And please, no emoticons.

☐ **Keep in mind that jokes can fall flat in
e-mail.** Avoid non-literal communications in
e-mails. Without the benefit of tone or body language, sarcasm and other non-literal communication is often misinterpreted in an e-mail.

Jokes that are misinterpreted—or not appreciated—can lead to awkward moments in the office—or even to discrimination claims.

☐ **Don't gossip or criticize colleagues in e-mail.** E-mails multiply like rabbits. Invariably, any denigrating remarks will end up in the wrong hands—and you will have no way to deny your authorship.

☐ **Reply to "Some."** The "Reply to All" button is one of the single biggest causes of e-mail annoyances and screw-ups. Use "Reply to All" judiciously. Few things are more annoying after a broadcast e-mail than getting dozens of responses that all say "thanks," "jacket was found," or "I am available." Some e-mail programs require you to confirm that you want to send an e-mail to a large group. This is a feature you should use.

☐ **Beware of the bcc.** If you blind copy someone in an e-mail and that person then uses "Reply to All," the other recipients may know that the person received the original e-mail.

☐ **Check the list.** Take the time to review the list of recipients. E-mail groups can be particularly dangerous because you generally do not see the names of each recipient—only the name of the group. Inadvertently including a third party in a client communication can destroy the attorney-client privilege. And e-mail trails that start out being innocuous can end up including highly sensitive information. Once, a general exchange about transportation issues developed into a discussion about how one firm would compete for an upcoming transportation project. The only problem was that lawyers from competing firms were still on the e-mail list.

☐ **Give yourself a second chance.** In some programs, such as Outlook, you can change the settings so that your e-mails are not sent instantaneously. Instead, they first go into an "outbox"

for an amount of time you specify, usually one or
two minutes. Those minutes can be a godsend if
you realize that you have just sent your grocery
list to every other lawyer in your firm. Instead
of getting smirks about the "personal care"
items on your list, you can simply go into the
outbox and delete the message: no harm; no
foul.

☐ **Make the buttons work for you.** If you find
you are too quick on the mouse and tend to hit
the "Send" or "Reply to All" buttons inadvertently, some e-mail programs allow you to move
the buttons to a different place on your toolbar
where they are less likely to cause mischief.
With some programs, an e-mail does not actually send until you *release* the mouse button. If
you realize you have made a mistake, you may
be able to move the mouse off the button and
then release it.

☐ **Remember: Recalling messages can compound your problems.** If you realize you have
hit "Send" accidentally, certain programs allow
you to recall unopened copies (but usually only
to internal recipients). You should make sure
you know how the feature works before you use
it. In some programs, the recall feature sends
out a new e-mail, indicating that you want to
recall the preceding one. When you do that,
you've been doubly annoying—before you have
even sent a corrected e-mail. And the feature
usually cannot recall messages from mobile
devices, so it's best not to screw up in the first
place.

☐ **Use "Auto Complete" with care.** The "Auto-
Complete" feature in many e-mail programs
saves keystrokes by suggesting a recipient for
your e-mail based on the first few characters
you type. As a result, the feature also enables
you to easily send a message to the wrong person. Either turn off "Auto-Complete" or use it
with caution.

☐ **Check your spelling.** It's easy to get sloppy precisely because e-mail is quick and efficient. But your e-mails to clients and colleagues should be letter-perfect every time. Set your e-mail program to automatically check your spelling, if that feature is available.

☐ **Delete the excess.** With lengthy e-mail strings, take care to delete any information that is not critical for your recipients. As e-mails bounce from person to person, getting longer and longer, someone may have included a snide remark that you unwittingly send to the person who is the subject of the remark. If your recipients need to see only the most recent exchange, delete the rest.

☐ **Reserve "hot" mail for your home computer.** The next tip seems obvious, but bears repeating: *Never* send sexually explicit communications using your business computer (and do not ever surf pornographic websites). That *includes* logging into a personal e-mail account using your work computer. Sexually explicit content is not only unprofessional, but also puts firms at risk for sexual harassment claims—even if someone just happens to see an image on your screen. Keep it clean. Keep your job. Also remember that your assistant (and anyone involved with Information Technology) may be able to read all of your e-mails.

☐ **Never forget: Your "personal" e-mail from work is not personal.** You should assume that the firm tracks all of your e-mail communication and Internet surfing—down to the keystroke.

☐ **Keep your work and personal e-mails separate.** Think twice before giving your work e-mail address to friends. You never know what might end up in your inbox.

NEVER LET THEM SEE YOU SWEAT

To inspire confidence in other lawyers, you need to display confidence. One lawyer was able to recover from the following fairly embarrassing situation by displaying confidence and a sense of humor:

An associate and several other lawyers had traveled to another city for a client meeting. They had all agreed to meet in the lobby of the hotel at 6:30 the next morning and then go to the client's offices for a 7 a.m. meeting. At 6:35 a.m., the associate's phone rang in his hotel room. It woke him up. The senior partner was on the other end of the line, asking him if he was coming down to the lobby. Rather than making up some story or keeping the other lawyers waiting (neither of which would have been good), he simply said, "I overslept, and I will meet you at the client's offices."

He got ready in a flash, caught a cab, and managed to make it to the client's offices minutes before the meeting started. When he arrived, his colleagues were gathered in a conference room. The senior partner stood up, and addressed the associate: "Jeff, I have some advice for you: Never oversleep, and never check your luggage."

Without missing a beat, the associate responded, "Oh, I would *never* check my luggage." All was forgiven, and the associate never overslept again.

Senior lawyers particularly expect you to be assertive with opposing lawyers. An associate had responded to a nasty letter from opposing counsel disputing the assertions—but without any bravado. After reading the response, the assigning lawyer handed it back. "It's too nice; you need to show your teeth."

When you correspond with opposing counsel, it is important to remember that you are also communicating to your client. If your client gets a nasty letter, the client usually expects you to hit back just as hard. If you don't, the client may think it has the wrong lawyer. Clients expect you to advocate vigorously on their behalf. Indeed, clients sometimes hire lawyers not because they have a reputation for being smart, but because they have a reputation for being tough—or worse. That doesn't mean you should be a jerk. It does mean you need to be assertive.

Similarly, in your communications with other attorneys, you cannot betray uncertainty, anxiety, or fear. You need to be able to defend the legal conclusions you have reached from rigorous scrutiny in the office—so they stand up under scrutiny outside the office. You must communicate with the confidence that comes from careful preparation. If you don't know the answer to a question, have the confidence to say that and then look it up. Few things are more painful than watching a new lawyer try to fake knowledge of a subject.

You must be able to handle the significant stress of juggling many high-stakes projects, meeting challenging deadlines, and doing superior legal work. Take steps to manage your stress, but do not let your colleagues see you buckle under pressure. If you need a time-out, take it behind closed doors.

CHAPTER 5

BECOMING A PILOT FISH: MAKING YOURSELF INDISPENSABLE WITH EXCEPTIONAL LEGAL WORK

ONLINE RESEARCH SKILLS: THE CASE OF THE ELUSIVE SUNDOME

You can quickly build your reputation by demonstrating superior legal research skills. Missing obvious legal authorities will have the opposite effect, as a lawyer in one sunny U.S. city learned.

The assignment was simple enough: "Did an amendment to a lease at the county-owned professional football stadium have to be approved by the county's legislative body?" It seemed to be one of those rare legal issues where there would actually be a clear "yes" or "no" answer. Surely, the senior lawyer thought, either the county code or state statutes dealt with the issue. The lawyer told the associate that he just needed a copy of the relevant statute.

The new lawyer ventured off into the land of electronic research. When a couple of days had gone by, the assigning attorney checked in. The stadium was known as the "Sundome," and the associate hadn't found anything that specifically addressed leases at the Sundome. The assigning lawyer said if there were no provisions on amending a lease, the associate should look for the procedures for *entering into* a lease. That had actually happened, and there had to be some process involved.

The associate continued his research for several more days. He found procedures for leases involving certain other county facilities—and general provisions involving leases—but nothing specifically related to leases at the stadium. He'd looked high and low—combing the county code and even state statutes.

The senior lawyer thought it was odd that there was no provision governing leases at the professional football stadium when there were code provisions for more mundane county buildings. Nonetheless, the associate insisted that he had looked at everything that could possibly be relevant. The senior lawyer became alarmed when the associate mentioned how much time he had spent on the project. After all, the question appeared to be very straightforward.

Since the associate had concluded that no legislation specifically addressed a lease at the Sundome, the assigning lawyer asked the associate to figure out which laws would apply and to write a memo explaining whether those laws would require the county legislative body to approve any lease amendment at the Sundome.

At this point, the associate had spent about ten times as long on the project as the senior lawyer had expected. There was still no answer, but of course, the firm could not tell the client, "Sorry, we can't figure this out." Anxiety was increasing on all fronts.

The associate dove back into the code provisions and decided that a general provision governing leases would also apply to leases at the stadium. Then he went about explaining why the provision applied and its impact on the proposal to amend the Sundome lease.

Meanwhile, the client was nagging the firm for an answer. The partner in charge replied that the issue seemed to be more complex than it initially appeared, but that the firm would have an answer very soon.

By the time the associate had completed the memo, he had racked up thousands of dollars in billable time—most of which could not be billed. After some fairly convoluted analysis, the memo concluded that an amendment to a lease at the Sundome did not need approval by the county commissioners.

The senior lawyer still had a nagging feeling that there had to be a code provision that specifically governed leases at the Sundome.

He went to his computer and logged in to the county code provisions. He typed in the word "stadium." The very first thing that came up was a code provision that in concise, direct, and unequivocal language stated that all leases and amendments to leases at the Sun County Domed Stadium had to be approved by the county commissioners. The lawyer groaned and groaned again when he found that the code contained an entire chapter of laws titled "Sun County Domed Stadium." He was dumbfounded—and angry. The associate had not found even one of these code sections—any one of which would have led to all the others.

Fortunately, the firm had not given the client an elaborate memo with the wrong answer. The firm did have to explain why it had taken so long to find a simple statute, and the firm did have to write off thousands of dollars' worth of time. That undoubtedly required extensive approvals, setting off alarm bells at the highest levels of management.

When the dust had settled, the senior attorney went to the associate to find out what had gone wrong—to find out how after hours and hours of research, the associate could have missed finding an entire chapter of laws devoted to the "Sun County Domed Stadium." He immediately had a simple answer: "I just kept using 'Sundome' in my searches."

PERFECTING YOUR ELECTRONIC RESEARCH SKILLS

Here are some tips to help you make a name for yourself by finding the authorities that elude other lawyers.

☐ Take advantage of online legal research training to learn about databases in your practice area and the strengths and weaknesses of various search techniques.

☐ Use reference attorneys from online research services. The attorneys are extremely knowledgeable about databases and search options and can also help you formulate searches.

☐   If in-house librarians are available, use them to start or confirm your research, but do not rely on them exclusively. You are responsible for making sure that your research is complete.

☐   Before you go online, spend some time thinking about the ways in which your concept could be expressed. Then search for the words that are critical for expressing that concept.

☐   Be careful to allow flexibility in your Boolean searches to account for variations in word order and parts of speech.

☐   Pare down your natural language searches. Including too many words can lead to unhelpful results.

☐   Start with general search terms and then narrow your research so that you do not exclude critical results. You can do broad searches and then use "locate" or "focus" commands to search more without an additional charge.

☐   Remember that terms of art can help you locate relevant authorities quickly, but some important authorities may address your issue without using the common monikers.

☐   Use head notes, key numbers, and citation services—all of which make searching less random.

☐   If an online table of contents is available, don't ignore it—it can help lead you to relevant authority quickly. With that in mind, don't be afraid to use actual books, which have not only tables of contents but also indices.

☐   Keep track of how various documents characterize your issue, and rephrase your queries accordingly.

☐   Start with the most relevant databases. If you find the answer from the best source, there may be no need to search through every case in the universe. Small databases are also usually less expensive.

☐ If you are searching statutes or regulations, make sure you understand the context in which you are searching. For example, if you find a provision on tax credits for oil wells, make sure you haven't ended up in a section on tax credits that does not apply to your state.

☐ Save your research so that you have a record of the legal authority that you reviewed.

☐ Make sure you understand how you are being charged for research services—and the way your firm bills for them. They may not be the same.

☐ Understand how to minimize the cost of particular searches—even if your firm has a contract for "unlimited" use. The cost of unlimited contracts is usually adjusted annually based on usage. The firm will care about the costs— particularly if it can't—or doesn't—bill clients for legal research services.

☐ Always, always, always make sure your authority is good law.

SHARPENING YOUR ANALYTICAL SKILLS

In law school, most legal analysis takes place in the context of law school exams or law review articles. Neither vehicle is particularly relevant to the real world. Law school exams are primarily issue-spotting exercises with little time for meticulous legal analysis. At the other end of the spectrum, law review articles may explore a topic virtually without end—delving deep into the minutiae. To succeed in the practice of law, most new lawyers need to sharpen their analytical skills so that they can provide legal advice that clients will pay for.

Senior lawyers generally have at least three common gripes about the analysis from most new lawyers. The first is that new lawyers go into a long dissertation of the law without applying the facts to answer the client's question. Jumping to unsupported conclusions is a related gripe. You have to *demonstrate* that your conclusions are correct, and frequently, new lawyers make assumptions that they do not even realize. The third gripe is that new associates' analyses are often muddled because they fail to winnow out irrelevant facts.

Summarizing all of the law that touches on your client's issue does the client little good. In fact, such a summary involves no analysis at all. The client needs you to understand the law and then apply the law to the relevant facts to provide an answer. If you begin your legal memos by succinctly answering the client's specific legal question, that should help force you to apply the most relevant facts to the law.

Not all facts are relevant, though, and there is a tendency for new lawyers to say something about every known fact. This is understandable because on law school exams, you usually get points for spotting as many issues as possible. There is no subtraction for mentioning something irrelevant. Thus the tendency to toss every detail into the analytical mix is often well ingrained by the end of law school. The habit is reinforced by new associates' fear about omitting something that a senior lawyer would consider important to the analysis. One way to make sure nothing important is left out is to include everything. But with that approach, results are less than optimal.

Tossing every known fact into the analytical mix serves only to cloud issues, not clarify them. It's like using the same amount of every ingredient in a recipe—and it results in prose that is usually a jumbled mess.

Clients and judges typically expect highly cogent analysis of only the most critical information. That means your job includes deciding what *not* to say. Statements that are not particularly persuasive tend to weaken your entire argument. Remember: Brevity is the soul of wit. The most compelling arguments are usually the most concise.

Start your analysis by deciding which facts are most critical to the outcome of the particular issue. Once you sort out those absolutely critical facts, making a logical, step-by-step argument becomes simpler. If you are having trouble seeing the forest for the trees, cut some trees.

After deciding what facts are critical to a particular outcome, you must meticulously establish that each and every one of those facts exists. This will help ensure that you do not jump to unsupported conclusions—one of the other frequent complaints about new lawyers' analyses. It is not enough for you to know—or God forbid, assume—that particular facts exist. You must *show* that those facts do—or don't—exist. Despite all the hammering on this point in law school, it is a frequent failing of new lawyers.

Particularly when dealing with statutes, new associates often fail to explain how their situation fits within the precise terms of the statute. In other words, they forget to explain exactly why the statute applies to the issue. Far too frequently, new lawyers simply assume that a statute applies and go from there. But if you have made an assumption that turns out to be wrong, your entire conclusion will unravel.

It may be useful to think of analysis like walking a tightrope. You must use extreme care to make sure that each step in your analysis follows logically from the previous step, leading the reader to your ultimate conclusion. Along the way, you must link each conclusion of law to the facts that support the conclusion. If you make any unsupported assumptions, you have gaps in your analysis, and the tightrope walker falls to his death.

Lawyers sometimes use linguistic crutches, such as "clearly," to make less than airtight arguments seem more persuasive. It doesn't work. Words like "clearly" and "obviously" do nothing to explain why a conclusion is correct. Those words serve primarily to highlight the fact that something isn't so obvious. If it were obvious, you wouldn't need to say it. A far better approach is to establish that all the key facts exist to compel your preferred legal result.

Regardless of your practice area, getting some experience writing legal briefs will help you hone your analytical skills. In pleadings, you generally have to place a citation after every declarative statement of fact or law. That is a good practice for all your writing. If you get in the habit of seeing whether you can place a citation after every statement of fact or law, your analysis will improve. With client memos, you often won't include all those references, but going through the exercise will help you make sure you haven't left any holes in your analysis.

Analytical Checklist

Considering these questions at the outset of a project should help make your analysis clear and cogent:

☐ What is the most concise statement of your legal question?

☐ What is the short answer to your client's question?

☐ What is the general rule or legal test for determining the outcome (that is, what is the law)?

☐ Are you sure you have the right legal test?

☐ Which facts are critical to the outcome of the test?

☐ Are there any other facts that cause an exception to apply?

☐ Why do the critical facts lead to a particular result under the general rule?

☐ (If applicable) Why do certain facts result in an exception to the general rule?

THE $1 MILLION COMMA AND OTHER PERILS OF FAILING TO PAY ATTENTION TO DETAIL

With everything else you have to learn as a new lawyer, it may seem daunting to produce perfect—or near perfect—work every time. But with legal work, the stakes are high. Clients and other lawyers can be unforgiving because seemingly small mistakes can be hugely expensive—or at least extremely embarrassing.

A firm was putting the finishing touches on an adult entertainment ordinance for a city that had grown tired of its red-light district. A final check of the ordinance uncovered typos that spell-check had missed (or perhaps had caused): "public" appeared in some places in the document where "pubic" was intended and vice versa. The errors resulted in such interesting phrases as "traditional pubic forum" and "pubic process." If the typos had gone uncorrected, the client would not have been amused.

Another client once told a new lawyer that he would fire any firm that sent him work containing typos. The new lawyer was shocked and asked for an explanation. The client replied, "I am paying a lot of money for your work, and there are lots of other law firms out there, so I want the work to be perfect." Although this perspective may be somewhat more demanding than the average client, clients do not expect to see typos in their work. And one of the easiest things clients can do is to stop calling.

If you think all this is overly demanding, consider whether you would buy an expensive new car that had small dents and scratches. And how forgiving you would be of typos on your law school diploma?

Typos can also be far more than an annoyance or embarrassment. The consequences of failing to pay attention to even tiny details can be grave as illustrated by the real-life case of the "million dollar comma." The story made the legal press across the globe. Here is the story as recounted by a law firm based in the United Kingdom:

> The position of a comma in a fourteen-page contract is at the heart of a dispute that could cost cable TV company Rogers Communications one million Canadian dollars.

> A five-year contract with Aliant Telecom gave Rogers access to thousands of poles that carried its cables to homes across Canada. Aliant didn't own the poles; it only acted as an agent for a power company. When the power company decided to take control of the poles itself and raise the rates, Aliant gave 12–months' notice to Rogers that its deal would be terminated one year before the expiry of the five-year term.

> Early termination would force Rogers to start paying the power company at the higher rates, costing Rogers an extra CAN$1 million over that final year. But Rogers could avoid this expense if Aliant had no right to terminate early.

> Aliant's right turned on a single clause:

> "[...This Agreement] shall be effective from the date it is made and shall continue in force for a period of five (5) years from the date it is made, and thereafter for suc-

cessive five (5) year terms, unless and until terminated by one year prior notice in writing by either party."

Based on the second comma, Aliant interpreted the contract as giving it a right to terminate at any time upon one year's notice to Rogers. Rogers read the clause as providing a right to terminate only at the end of the current or a renewed five-year term.

This case illustrates how careful you have to be in selecting words and even punctuation, and in double-checking your work. The stakes can be very high.

Cutting corners in reviewing legal authorities also causes trouble. In a misguided attempt to be efficient, new lawyers sometimes read only a portion of applicable cases—or do not read the actual case at all. This limits learning and can lead to mistakes, as illustrated in this story about an associate on the East Coast who was overly "efficient."

The associate's memo reached a conclusion that the assigning lawyer thought was surprising. Although there was some contrary authority, the new lawyer had found a case directly on point and cited the holding. The assigning lawyer noticed that there was no pinpoint citation and asked to see the case. It turned out that the case held exactly the opposite of what the associate had written in the memo. When asked about the problem, the associate pointed to a head note from the case that he had cut and pasted into the memo. Comparing the head note to the actual ruling in the case uncovered the problem: Somehow the word "not" had ended up in the head note—but the word wasn't in the corresponding ruling in the actual case. The associate had read only the head note, resulting in a memo that was completely wrong.

Undoubtedly there was delay, time was written off, and the associate probably got a reputation for being sloppy.

Even when mistakes are caught and corrected, they can damage an associate's reputation. New lawyers sometimes mistakenly believe that more senior lawyers are supposed to check their work and catch their mistakes. In fact, the opposite is true. Over time, senior lawyers will want to depend on you to make sure *their* work is accurate. Usually, the senior lawyer's primary job is to manage work and client relations.

More experienced lawyers will look at your analysis to see whether it makes sense in light of what they know about the law. But they don't have time to check the accuracy or completeness of all your research, citations, and the like. Since they can't check all of your work, if they find any mistakes, they will assume that there are other mistakes and that they cannot send your work to a client without checking everything. If senior lawyers have to do that, there is little point in having your "help" on the project.

Senior lawyers want to be able to review your work and send it directly to the client—with as few changes as possible. Thus, *all* of your work needs to be as perfect as you can make it.

Tips for Keeping Errors at Bay

The following checklist (and lots of focus) should help you produce error-free work:

- ☐ Get in the habit of asking clients for the spelling and pronunciation of any name that you don't know for certain—and then double-check. "Bobbie Faucette" is probably not spelled the way you expect. "Jean" is not "Gene," "MacLean" is not "McClain," "Stuart" is not "Stewart," and "Delta Air Lines" is not "Delta Airlines." If you do notice that you've misspelled someone's name, take the initiative to apologize.

- ☐ Be extra careful about checking information that has an obvious right or wrong answer. The perfect adjective to describe the opposing party may be debatable. The total from multiplying two numbers is not debatable.

- ☐ Be sure to quote cases and other authority exactly. If you don't cite accurately, you cannot expect anyone to trust your interpretation of the legal authorities.

- ☐ Use pinpoint cites and double-check all of them. That's a good way to force yourself to quote material exactly.

☐ Don't put information into documents until you verify its accuracy. It's better to leave a blank and then add the information after you confirm that it is correct. Alternatively, include the information with brackets or some other obvious notation that will remind you to verify the information before finalizing the document. This approach can be dangerous, though. Particularly with large documents, you run the risk of sending out the document with inaccurate information—highlighted by your notation to "check this."

☐ Never assume that information you receive is correct. If the information is important, you should verify it independently.

☐ Double-check section references in contracts and other documents. The references are likely to change as the documents evolve.

☐ Whenever possible, cut and paste information into a document rather than having it retyped.

☐ Be careful when using the "Auto-Correct" and "Spell-Check" features. The "corrections" you get may not be the ones you want.

☐ Don't ever, ever guess. Always look things up. The worst thing you can do is say that you know what the answer is—only to be proved wrong later. It is far better to say that you don't know for certain, but will find the answer.

☐ Use the firm's resources to help make your documents accurate—check your conclusions with other associates, have support staff make any major edits to your documents, and if available, use the firm's editors and proofreaders.

☐ Buy and read Strunk and White's *The Elements of Style*.

☐ Do not rely on a "draft" notation to submit less than perfect work. Putting "draft" on a document *may* provide some leeway to do additional formatting; it provides no clemency for errors.

- ☐ If you need to compare two hard copies of a document to see whether one has been changed, you can place each page from both documents on top of one another and hold them up to the light to see whether they match. You can also compare the last letter of every line in both documents.

- ☐ Send documents in PDF format to prevent changes that you do not know about.

- ☐ Always do a final review of documents yourself. Ultimately, you are responsible for the work.

CHAPTER 6

NAVIGATING THE CURRENTS: MANAGING AND BUILDING YOUR PRACTICE

TAMING TIME

The reward for doing a good job at law firms is more work. If you are fortunate, there will be days when you are completely overwhelmed.

As a new lawyer, time management is likely to be one of your biggest challenges. Work does not come into the office in uniform chunks. It is also difficult to estimate how long projects will take, and new projects can pop up all the time. There are days when you may face a swarm of competing projects, deadlines, calls to return, and facts to check—and double-check.

When you get overwhelmed, the first thing you must do is *slow down*. That seems counter-intuitive, and you may have a very difficult time doing it, but slowing down is essential. Get to the office early in the morning before things become frenetic; leave the office for fifteen minutes and visit a coffee shop—do whatever works for you, but when everything reaches the boiling point, stop and take stock. This will help you keep critical tasks from falling through the cracks.

When you feel completely buried, it is more important than ever to have an hour-by-hour or day-by-day plan for attacking the work. Taking a few minutes to clear your head can save you literally hours of time—and will help keep you from forgetting critical deadlines.

Taking time to come up with a plan to get your work done can also relieve the anxiety of worrying about how to get it all done. The simple act of listing your projects and prioritizing what absolutely has to be done can have a calming effect by itself. You may find that things are not as dire as they seemed. You may find that there are several tasks that you can delegate. In any event, attacking projects with a plan will help you get them done more efficiently.

As you gain more experience, you'll have a better idea of how long projects will take—and when to ask for new work. But because the goal at law firms is to make sure everyone is always busy, managing your time is always important.

Overcoming the Overwhelming

Here are some tips to get your work under control on an overwhelming day:

- [ ] Breathe. Despite what happens, no one will die (usually).

- [ ] Make a list of everything you absolutely have to get done that day and approximately how long you think it will take—or at least how long you can spend on each project and still get it all done in time.

- [ ] Go over the list and see what tasks—or portions of tasks—you can delegate to someone else. It helps to notify others as soon as possible that you will need assistance so that they can set aside time to help.

- [ ] Prioritize the tasks that you absolutely must do yourself. It may help to schedule specific tasks for specific times of the day.

- [ ] Add longer term tasks to the end of the list, and try to delegate portions of those so that you can get back in control as soon as possible. If you have a document due in a few days, see whether a paralegal can track down some needed information while you are buried on other projects.

- [ ] Put your list in a prominent place so that you can easily refer to it on the fly.

MANAGING YOUR WORK FLOW

Managing your work flow is important even when there is no crisis. Here are some tips to keep projects moving.

☐ **Plan daily.** Take the time every morning to plan your work day. This helps you prioritize what has to be done. Then communicate with your assistant about the administrative time you need. Figure out ways to keep each project moving forward (for example, by delegating certain tasks).

☐ **Use an electronic calendar.** Keep your appointments and tasks in an electronic calendar that you and your assistant can easily update.

☐ **Check in.** To help with planning, regularly ask lawyers how much of your time they expect to need in the upcoming days and weeks.

☐ **Say "no."** If you have a plan to complete work over the next week, you know whether or not you can take on more big projects. If you truly cannot take on more work without compromising the quality, it is important to say so. (One caveat: You should rarely (if ever) turn down work from a lawyer with whom you want to build an ongoing working relationship.) A senior lawyer's temporary disappointment is far better than having to cut corners and getting a reputation for sloppy work. When you need to say "no," practice diplomacy. First, thank the lawyer for the offer of work. Then offer an explanation— "Unfortunately, it does not look like I can possibly get to this until late next week"—rather than an abrupt "No."

☐ **Ask for specific deadlines.** When a senior lawyer tells you "as soon as you can," that is not particularly helpful. Get the specifics.

☐ **Set numerous reminders well in advance.** A default fifteen-minute reminder in Outlook is not enough time to draft a brief or a contract.

☐ **Develop useful routines.** Routines help. Plan around the time of day that you are most productive. If you are a morning person, dive into the complex work right away and leave the administrative tasks for later in the day. Handling routine matters at the same time every day can help ensure they don't fall through the cracks.

☐ **Delegate.** Use support staff as much as possible. That will free up time to focus on legal work—the work you were hired to do. Doing non-legal work keeps you from progressing as a lawyer.

☐ **Eat your peas first.** If you tend to procrastinate, commit to spending the first fifteen minutes of each day working on a project that you have been putting off. After you start, you may find the project is not as horrible as you thought. Since projects rarely go away, it's better to put your energy into starting rather than fretting.

☐ **Eat your peas a little at a time.** As time passes, an unpleasant project usually becomes even more difficult because you forget details, lose information, or have to start and finish it under extreme deadline pressure. Overcoming procrastination is primarily about *starting* a project. Break large projects into many small tasks and commit to doing a few of those tasks every day.

☐ **Set a time-limit and move on.** If you get bogged down on a particular project, give yourself a time limit for that particular issue. When the time is up, move on to something else and come back to the project later. You may have an epiphany in the meantime (or at least a fresh perspective).

☐ **Expect the unexpected.** Allow some time in your day for unexpected projects and for projects that take longer than you expect. You can also expect deadlines to get moved up.

☐ **Don't be the bottleneck.** Block out some time each day to keep small projects moving off your desk—even if you are swamped on huge projects. Some projects can be completed in the amount of time it would take you to tell the client you haven't completed them. Clear those off your desk as soon as possible.

☐ **Start early or stay late—or both.** You can often get your most productive work accomplished before or after most people are in the office, that quiet time when the barrage of phone calls and e-mails has abated.

☐ **Beat your deadlines.** Sooner is better than later. Give yourself a deadline to finish projects that is before the actual deadline. The deadline is not the only date you can finish a project; it is just the last possible date.

☐ **Focus on finishing.** If you start the week by doing a little work on five projects each day and finish them all on Friday, you have kept five people waiting five days for their projects. But if you finish one project each day, you keep fewer people waiting.

☐ **Ask for help.** If two major projects are careening toward the same impossible deadline, ask your practice group leader or another senior lawyer for help in resolving time conflicts. Do this *well before* there is a crisis.

☐ **Complete time entries daily.** Tracking your time is a critical part of doing work at most firms (some might say the *most* critical part). If you put off recording your time, you will have to spend much more non-billable time trying to remember what you did on a particular day and your time entries are less likely to be accurate. Clients do not like to see bills that show two lawyers attending the same meeting on different days.

☐ **Deal with each paper or e-mail only once.** Reading a letter, drafting a response, and filing the letter right away is far more efficient than reading it, putting it down, misplacing it on your desk, looking for it, finding it, re-reading it, starting to work on a response, stopping, finding the letter again, reading it again, starting the response again ... enough said.

☐ **Stay organized.** Looking for misplaced documents and information is one of the more stressful and unproductive endeavors in the practice of law.

Controlling Interruptions

Particularly if you are working on many small projects, you may find yourself assailed by countless interruptions. Here are some tips to help you complete your work, despite the competing demands for your attention:

☐ **Leave.** If you need uninterrupted time to work, close your door, ask your assistant to tell people not to interrupt you, put a "do not disturb" note on your door, or leave and work from somewhere besides your office. Do whatever you need to get your work done; just make sure you can be reached in a crisis.

☐ **Hold those calls.** The phone can be a constant source of interruption that prevents you from prioritizing your day. Try to handle calls during blocks of time during the day. For at least a couple of hours every day, let calls roll to voicemail or silence the ringer. If there are a few people you must speak with, ask your assistant to answer your calls.

☐ **Turn off e-mail notifications.** It's easy to want to respond to e-mails as soon as they arrive. But if you do, every e-mail becomes more important than anything else you are doing at the moment. In other words, your e-mail is in control of your schedule—not you. Turn off intrusive e-mail notifications, and respond to e-mails during blocks of time that work best for you.

☐ **Don't let social butterflies land for long.** Social butterflies are a fairly rare species among lawyers, but they do exist. In extreme cases, they can cause you to have to work late, skip lunch, or come in extra early. You should build friendships at the office—but not at the expense of your work. Here are three approaches that should keep the butterflies moving:

1. "I am really enjoying this conversation; let's continue it when we both have more time";

2. "I should let *you* get back to work"; or for the truly dense:

3. "I'm sorry, but I really need to get back to this project."

☐ **Check in with clients.** Regularly check in with the lawyers and clients for whom you are doing work. If you don't call them, they will call you, and you are better off checking in when it is convenient for you.

Building a More Civilized Practice

Here are some tips to help you build a practice that you enjoy and can sustain over the long term:

☐ **Be picky—when possible.** Try to avoid taking work from disorganized partners who have constant last-minute crises, and work to build relationships with organized lawyers who respect your time. Lawyers who treat you as a limitless commodity are also unlikely to stand up for you when discussions about bonuses or layoffs arise.

☐ **Prioritize to build relationships.** Many associates prioritize tasks based solely on the deadline. The deadline is a vital consideration, but with careful planning, you can also prioritize based on the lawyers with whom you would most like to work or the lawyers who are most likely to stand up for you and give you a good performance review.

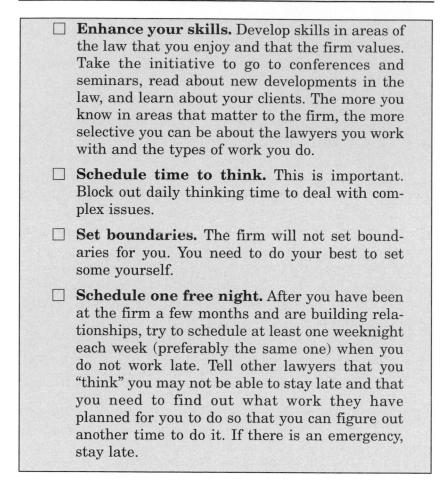

☐ **Enhance your skills.** Develop skills in areas of the law that you enjoy and that the firm values. Take the initiative to go to conferences and seminars, read about new developments in the law, and learn about your clients. The more you know in areas that matter to the firm, the more selective you can be about the lawyers you work with and the types of work you do.

☐ **Schedule time to think.** This is important. Block out daily thinking time to deal with complex issues.

☐ **Set boundaries.** The firm will not set boundaries for you. You need to do your best to set some yourself.

☐ **Schedule one free night.** After you have been at the firm a few months and are building relationships, try to schedule at least one weeknight each week (preferably the same one) when you do not work late. Tell other lawyers that you "think" you may not be able to stay late and that you need to find out what work they have planned for you to do so that you can figure out another time to do it. If there is an emergency, stay late.

PREPARING FOR THE
FIVE O'CLOCK SHUFFLE

You need to determine the administrative support you will need well ahead of time and delegate those tasks early so that when the "five o'clock shuffle" arrives, you are out of the fray.

The five o'clock shuffle usually begins about 4:30 in the afternoon. Three lawyers who share the same assistant all realize they have to send out documents within half an hour. They simultaneously rush to their assistant's workstation and frantically insist on edits to documents, photocopies, labels, PDF files—and sometimes tasks far more extreme. Despite being overwhelmed, the assistant ignores her ulcer, performs minor miracles, makes a hand-off to the overnight delivery service, and rushes out the door to start a long commute.

At law offices, though, miracles don't come in threes. The assistant handles the senior lawyer's project entirely and completely, and the lawyer goes back to talking with clients. The assistant also handles as many of the mid-level associate's tasks as possible. That leaves the new lawyer. She is lucky even to score a mailing label from the melee. For the new lawyer, the five o'clock shuffle becomes the five o'clock brush-off.

The Office Support You Need

The five o'clock shuffle holds these lessons for new lawyers:

☐ **Learn how work gets prioritized.** Learn how work gets prioritized in your office so that yours gets done on time. Staff members are likely to prioritize work for senior lawyers over junior lawyers, so you may want to mention that the senior lawyer requested the project. Most word-processing departments complete work in the order of the stated deadline; if you specify a deadline of 6 a.m., your work is likely to get completed before all of the projects with an 8 a.m. deadline. Whatever the process, you have to figure out the system and make it work for you. One attorney had an assistant who had an "in box" for projects and pulled work *only* from the bottom of the pile. Whenever the attorney had a rush project, he put his work at the very bottom of the stack.

☐ **Plan ahead.** It is far more important for you to coordinate your work with your assistant than for senior lawyers to do so. Poor planning on your part won't constitute an emergency on anyone's part. So meet briefly with your assistant every morning to go over the tasks that you might need help on that day. Be as specific as possible about the assistance you need and when you expect to need it.

☐ **If necessary, develop "Plan B."** You should also confirm that your assistant will be able to help. If you find out in the morning that your assistant is booked solid for the day, it is far easier for the two of you to make other arrangements to complete the work in an orderly manner. With notice, your assistant should find someone else to get the job done on time. You should also be aware of back-up resources that are available at your office, such as word-processing or photocopying departments.

☐ **Maintain control.** You may occasionally encounter an assistant who tries to deflect work—particularly from new lawyers—despite plenty of lead time. That is not acceptable. Lawyer billing rates are too high for lawyers to do administrative work—except in an unusual crisis. If you have given plenty of lead time and still get push-back, here is an approach that may work: "I am sorry, but we can't bill the client for administrative tasks, so I need you to find someone else who can help out with this."

☐ **Be self-sufficient in a pinch.** As a new lawyer, you need to be relatively self-sufficient so that you can edit letters, print documents, create PDF files, electronically file court documents, and perform other administrative tasks *in a crisis*. This should not, of course, become a habit. Clients cringe at the thought of a pricey lawyer standing at a photocopy machine. They won't want to pay for all the time it takes you to do a project *and* the associated administrative tasks.

SUPERVISION 101: GETTING THE MOST OUT OF YOUR ASSISTANT

Practicing law requires teamwork. Some new lawyers believe that if they build good relations with other lawyers, they don't need to worry about being nice to staff. That's a big mistake. The support staff at the firm can have a huge impact on your career. In a crisis, the last thing you need is an assistant being passive-aggressive about completing your documents.

Communicating your expectations clearly, holding your assistant accountable, and above all, being respectful are critical to a productive working relationship. Unfortunately, that is often easier said than done, particularly for new lawyers without experience supervising others.

New lawyers are sometimes frustrated that their assistants aren't meeting their expectations. The reasons are varied, but the problem often lies with the lawyer—not the assistant. Sometimes the lawyer's expectations are not realistic; more commonly, they are not clearly communicated. Assistants can rarely meet expectations that aren't communicated. You should seek out the help of other lawyers to develop and communicate clear expectations for your assistant. You should also involve your assistant in the process. She knows much more about the job than you do—at least at first—and can also provide invaluable information on ways in which the two of you can work together most effectively. Moreover, your assistant will also appreciate being involved in the process.

Some firms have lawyers fill out forms that address basic aspects of the assistant's work (also known as desk instructions). The forms cover such things as how phone calls and filing should be handled. The forms are not particularly useful as a communication tool—an ongoing dialogue is preferable. But the forms can serve as a starting point for your discussion, and they are an efficient way for an assistant who is filling in to understand the lawyers' preferences (or idiosyncrasies) about administrative functions. At first, you may not know how you want your assistant to handle various functions, and your preferences may change over time. If you aren't certain, or if something isn't working well, your best sources of advice are the other lawyers who work with your assistant—and your assistant, herself.

If you think your assistant has made a mistake, you must hold him accountable by calling it to his attention as soon as possible. Unfortunately, some associates fly off the handle when mistakes occur. They don't realize that holding someone accountable and meting out punishment are very different.

Your assistant is a highly trained professional and should *always* be treated with respect. Law firms are high-stress environments, and you only compound problems by blowing your top. You will also be sending the inadvertent message to other lawyers that you can't act professionally under stress. It is never appropriate to become belligerent or to criticize your assistant in front of others. Both are demoralizing and do more harm than good—despite the fact that you may see some senior lawyers engage in these behaviors.

A new lawyer who was finishing a clerkship was a shoo-in for a prestigious job. He had the right connections and references, the initial interviews had gone very well, and the final interview seemed a mere formality. Paperwork was involved, of course, and that required the help of the lawyer's secretary. The lawyer was not happy with the documents, and he berated his secretary, as was his habit. She usually just sucked it up. But this time was different. Having been a legal secretary for more than twenty years, she was also well connected. She made a call to a friend who worked for the lawyer's prospective employer. Soon thereafter, the job that was a sure-thing was no longer available. The lesson is simple: Treat everyone with respect. It's the right thing to do, and you never know where people will end up.

If you have repeated problems with an assistant—or even other attorneys—discuss the situation with a senior lawyer in your practice area or with human resources staff. You need to deal with problems immediately, but do give your assistant the benefit of the doubt. Everyone makes honest mistakes on occasion, and your assistant is likely to know much more about the firm than you do. There is a possibility that your assistant didn't make a mistake—or that you made a request that was not consistent with firm policy.

The best way to hold your assistant accountable will depend on the situation. A good approach might be something like "I may not have been clear, but ... " This lets the assistant know that you identified the problem and that, although you are not placing blame, he needs to resolve it. If you are not sure whether your assistant made a mistake, a statement such as, "This doesn't look right to me" gives you some wiggle-room if you are wrong.

If your assistant misses a few edits you have marked on a document, a response like, "Thanks for your help on this; I noticed that there are still a couple more edits that I need you to make" will communicate that you appreciate the work but that it was not quite up to par. If a similar mistake happens fairly soon afterwards, say something like, "I need you to double-check these before you return them to me because I noticed a few things that were missed." Whatever you say, be respectful, and make sure your assistant is the one who corrects the problem.

It may seem that your assistant tries to get away with things for you that he would not try with a more seasoned attorney. Infractions can run the gamut, but trying to deflect work and missing deadlines are among the more common problems. If you have confirmed with other lawyers in advance that your expectations are reasonable and you have communicated those expectations clearly to your assistant (in writing, if necessary), you are likely to have fewer problems. You are also likely to have fewer problems if you bring mistakes to your assistant's attention—the first time and every time.

If problems continue, communicate by e-mail so that you have a record of your communications with the assistant. Copying a more senior lawyer may be enough to resolve the situation because it provides a gentle reminder that a project is not just for "the new guy." But don't overdo it; be respectful of the senior lawyer's time.

Of course, you have to adjust your approach to each situation, and other lawyers at the firm can give you tips. But the main lessons here are that you bring mistakes to your assistant's attention and you do so respectfully. If you catch mistakes that your assistant has made and you simply correct them without saying anything, you are not holding your assistant accountable. You are also inadvertently sending one or more of the following messages: Your assistant is not making mistakes; you don't mind correcting your assistant's mistakes; or you don't care about mistakes. Those are not messages that lead to high-quality work.

The Invaluable Assistant

A good working relationship with your primary support staff will make your life at the firm much easier. Keep these tips in mind:

☐ Work with your assistant to figure out the ways he can best support your practice.

☐ Plan ahead. Give your assistant as much notice as possible about tasks for which you may need help. Emergencies will not endear you to your assistant.

☐ Know how tasks break down at your firm. Typical tasks for an assistant include:

  ○ Managing your calendar

  ○ Opening and sorting mail

  ○ Answering your phone

  ○ Making contact lists of the key players on major transactions

  ○ Maintaining organized files

  ○ Editing documents

  ○ Distributing documents

  ○ Organizing cases and documents into binders

  ○ Assisting with time-entry

☐ Never ask your assistant to handle personal matters such as your household errands or bills.

☐ Remember that your assistant is not your therapist and vice versa. Don't engage in firm gossip with your assistant or try to be best friends. Maintain a professional relationship at all times.

☐ Set clear expectations, and hold your assistant accountable.

☐ If you have repeated problems with an assistant, ask another attorney for advice.

☐ Be respectful. Staff members have a number of choices when they come across a potential error in your work. They can fix the error, discuss the error with you, or ignore the error. The way you treat staff members is likely to affect their choices.

☐ Thank your assistant and other support staff regularly.

☐ Remember your assistant's birthday and Administrative Professionals' Day.

☐ Refer to your assistant by any reasonable title that your assistant prefers. Some are fine with the term "secretary"; others cringe.

☐ Introduce your assistant to clients.

☐ Include staff in celebrations on large transactions or litigation victories.

☐ Project enthusiasm about your work. You can't expect your assistant to have a positive attitude if you don't.

MAKING YOUR MARK WITH PRESENTATIONS

Making presentations is one of the primary ways that lawyers market their services to other lawyers and clients and gain a reputation as experts in a particular field. It won't be long before a senior lawyer asks you to assist in drafting material for a presentation that she has agreed to give. This is a very good way to learn a new area of the law. Put your name on the presentation as co-author (even though you will probably be the primary author) so that you get credit for your work and begin to build your own reputation. If a senior lawyer is reluctant to share credit, you should be assertive and ask. When your name appears on a presentation, participants are likely to call with questions or to get additional information—even months later.

Perform well, and you will soon be tagged to make a presentation yourself. Because of last-minute scheduling conflicts, you may also find yourself at the podium even sooner than you expect. There are two important things to remember: (1) just by having done the research, you know more about a topic than most of your audience members, and (2) no one is out to get you. Every lawyer was a new lawyer once and should be able to empathize with you.

Before you present, practice, practice, practice, and then try to relax and just do your best.

Public Speaking Tips

Here are a few tips that should ensure your presentation goes well:

- ☐ Make sure the technology is working in advance.

- ☐ Know your presentation software well.

- ☐ Have a back-up copy of your presentation close by.

- ☐ Prepare, prepare, prepare. This is the best way to deal with presentation anxiety. Keep in mind that if you have spent significant time researching a topic, you probably know more about it than most people in the room—even lawyers who have practiced far longer.

- ☐ If the presentation is broadcast or recorded, make sure that your voice is picked up on the microphone and that you stay in the frame of the camera.

- ☐ Start your presentation by telling the audience the key points you plan to make, address those points in greater detail, and then summarize the points you made.

- ☐ Use a limited number of slides.

- ☐ Use bullets, and limit the number of words on a slide. Paragraphs of text on a slide are mind-numbing and often illegible from the back of a room. Put detail in an accompanying paper.

- ☐ Elaborate on the information in your slides, but don't read from your slides. Reading slides verbatim quickly causes the audience to tune out.

- ☐ Make your presentation interactive to keep audience members engaged, and include real-life examples that will be relevant to them.

- ☐ Make speaking notes for each slide in large type. That way, if you get stuck, you can simply glance down, read your notes, and make your point.

☐ If you are anxious about the number of people in the audience, try to focus on just a few of them and block out the rest—or just try to focus on the back of the room and pretend that the audience is not there at all.

☐ Do not worry if some people tune out. For better or worse, seminar attendees often surf the Internet, catch up on reading, or do billable work.

☐ Remind yourself that in about thirty minutes your presentation will be over—no matter what. Nothing truly horrible can happen in thirty minutes, particularly when you have a script.

☐ Avoid gimmicks and excessive humor. As a young lawyer, you want to highlight your preparation, competence, and professionalism. Later on, with more experience, you can develop a personal style.

☐ Do a dry run of your entire presentation in front of a mirror, and time yourself. This will highlight areas that might cause you to stumble.

☐ Anticipate questions so that you have concise responses ready for the most logical questions.

☐ If audience members asking questions do not have a microphone, repeat the question for the rest of the audience and any recording.

☐ If you get a question you can't answer, don't guess or apologize. Just say you aren't certain or haven't dealt with that situation, and ask if anyone in the audience knows the answer. That's far better than guessing and being wrong, and audience members usually love to share their own opinions and experiences.

☐ Give yourself a break. You are a new lawyer and aren't expected to know everything.

CHAPTER 7

SHARK SUPPLY: LAW FIRM ECONOMICS

FASTEST IS CHEAPEST

For new lawyers, the unique nature of law firm economics often requires a shift in thinking about the best way to get things done. As a new lawyer, your time is suddenly very valuable—or at least very expensive.

The cost of legal services can lead to some seemingly strange outcomes. For example, paying a small fortune to use the business center in an airport is usually worthwhile if it enables you to accomplish any work. Likewise, the fastest mode of transportation usually turns out to be the cheapest overall when you add in the cost to the client of billing travel time.

Right out of law school, just a few minutes of your time may cost $100 or so. Charging that much for time takes some getting used to—and changes the decisions you might ordinarily make. Suddenly *anything* that allows you to do more billable work is usually worth the cost. Since flying is faster, the combined cost of your travel time and an airplane flight is most often cheaper for the client than the cost of driving and the additional travel time.

One new associate had landed at the airport and was on his way to a client meeting. Just as he had gotten his luggage, he saw the public bus arrive that was headed for downtown. He did a quick calculation in his head and decided he could save the client some money. The cost of bus fare compared to a cab ride was a no-brainer. He hopped on the bus and only then realized his mistake as the bus s-l-o-w-l-y made its way into the city. The bus took more than an hour to get into downtown from the airport. A taxi would have taken only about half an hour. The associate told the firm to write off the time for the slow bus ride and stopped taking buses.

TIME IS MONEY

When you first begin practicing law, your primary focus needs to be on the quality of your work. If you do high-quality work, you will get more work. But law firms are also businesses. In addition to doing high-quality work, you must eventually be profitable. At law firms that bill by the hour, time literally is money. One of the primary goals at any firm is to make money—preferably lots of money. Some new lawyers do not appreciate the importance of generating revenue, even though they regularly receive direct deposits in their bank accounts.

Your orientation on the topic of money is likely to go something like this: The discussion will start with the importance of tracking time. A senior partner is likely to remind you to track your time carefully and tell you that you do not have any authority to record less time than a project actually took to complete. That statement is likely to be repeated: You do not have any *authority* to record less time than you spent on a project.

If you think you have been inefficient or if you run into problems on a project, you are likely to hear that the only acceptable approach is to record all the time you spent and notify the assigning attorney. This is sound advice because when you first start out, you do not have any experience determining how long projects should take and running into unexpected issues on a project is a common occurrence.

As if the time-tracking message needed reiterating, the next discussion on the topic of money is likely to involve firm overhead. You will probably hear that the firm's overhead is very high, with expensive office space, extensive support staff, high-tech equipment, and associate salaries. You may also hear that it takes several months or longer for associates to "break even" because of their high salaries and the firm's other overhead expenses.

These high fixed costs account for the billable-hours requirements. It takes significant revenue to cover the firm's costs, and those costs must be paid before the partners earn a dime.

With all this emphasis on tracking time, it is puzzling that some associates simply do not make the connection between billing time and the firm's ability to stay in business. Sometimes it seems like a pain to track and record all your time. Sometimes you just lose track. Sometimes it seems unfair to the client. Sometimes you just don't feel like working. Regardless of the reason, failing to meet your billable-hours requirements is an easy one-way ticket out the door.

You are likely to find that partners have little tolerance for associates who do not take their work commitments seriously. Consider the perspective of a partner who took pride in spending significant time mentoring new lawyers. She observed that several associates who had not met their billable-hours requirements had taken off the last two weeks of the year. They figured that even if they worked those two weeks, they would not meet their hours requirements, so there was no point in sticking around. This was her reaction:

> Taking two weeks off when you have decided you can't make your hours or deciding that a lack of work is the firm's problem and not the associate's problem makes me crazy. Do something. Write a CLE paper, a marketing article, or learn a new area of the law. Do something, because you need to learn and you are being paid. I looked for associates to help at the end of the year, and most of them were gone. I have a long memory.

In the same vein, you need to make sure that it does not appear that you worked less than you actually did. It is not uncommon for associates to lament that they did not record all of their time because they thought the projects took a long time and they did not want to bill all of that time to the client. Then the associates lament having to make up the time by doing even more work.

Deciding not to record all of your time is misplaced magnanimity. As a new lawyer, you do not have any perspective on the amount of time that is appropriate for particular projects. In addition, the client did not ask for a gift. You aren't even telling the client about your gift. Yet you are essentially giving up your vacation time (or cutting the partners' pay) by not recording all your billable hours. Don't do it. With a little "generosity," you can end up with an hours deficit that you can never overcome.

Miracles Are Not Free

If giving up your vacation time isn't enough, here are a few more thoughts to consider if you are tempted to shave your time.

☐ Your firm pays you handsomely to perform miracles for clients. Do your level best to perform those miracles, and also do your level best to make sure the firm gets paid for those miracles.

☐ Encountering some challenges in completing a project is not uncommon for any lawyer and is just part of the process of coming up with the right answer.

☐ As a new lawyer, your billing rate is set relatively low to reflect the fact you won't be as efficient as more experienced lawyers. If you could complete projects more quickly, your billing rate would be higher.

☐ New lawyers don't have much frame of reference for how long projects should take or how much they should cost. What you think is an exorbitant bill may seem miniscule to more seasoned lawyers—and to clients.

☐ If you think that a client should not have to pay for a certain task—or should pay less, record the time and then talk to the assigning attorney about not billing a portion of the time. You can suggest how much you think should be written off.

☐ Meeting the firm's stated billable-hours requirement is important, but it may not be enough. At some firms you may be considered a slacker if you don't exceed the firm's official standard. Check with other associates to see whether there is an unstated billable-hours expectation.

☐ You don't have to be in the office to work. Sometimes it is just more palatable to bring work home. Just don't forget to record the time.

All of the emphasis on tracking your *actual* time does *not* mean that you should double-bill—that is, bill two clients for the same increment of time. There *may* be some gray areas related to this issue, so check on your firm's policy. However, the unequivocal perspective of the American Bar Association is that double billing is *verboten*:

> A lawyer who spends four hours of time on behalf of three clients has not earned twelve billable hours. A lawyer who flies for six hours for one client, while working for five hours on behalf of another, has not earned eleven billable hours. A lawyer who is able to reuse old work product has not re-earned the hours previously billed and compensated when the work product was first generated. Rather than looking to profit from the fortuity of coincidental scheduling, the desire to get work done rather than watch a movie, or the luck of being asked the identical question twice, the lawyer who has agreed to bill solely on the basis of time spent is obliged to pass the benefits of these economies on to the client. Model Rule 1.5. ABA Formal Opinion 93–379 at 7.

A rule of karma is also worth considering in these situations: "Pigs get fat; hogs get slaughtered."

TIME RECORDS: MAKING YOUR BILLABLE TIME MORE BILLABLE

Recording time is one of the most dreaded aspects of practicing law at most firms. It is also one of the most important. If you find that it is easy to compartmentalize your life in increments of a few minutes, you should consider yourself lucky—in some ways. For everyone else, accurate timekeeping takes constant diligence—despite computer programs and timers that help automate the process.

Most associates know to pay close attention to the *amount* of time they spend on projects. They spend less time—often as little as possible—thinking about how they describe the services they provide. That can be a mistake. Bills are the one regular communication that clients get from your firm. Bills summarize all the work the firm did for the client in the preceding month. The cost of those services is always obvious on a bill. The value of those services needs to be just as obvious.

For the most part, clients won't know exactly what you did for them—and they may not care. What clients do care deeply about is whether the work gave them any benefit. Clients don't see the late nights you put in at the office. They aren't there when you find the seminal case that will save them scads of money. They aren't with you when you come up with the legal theory that solves their problem. In other words, clients may not understand the benefits of your services unless you tell them.

Clients are rarely shy about asking for a write-off if they think fees are excessive, but firms can work to prevent such uncomfortable discussions by trimming the fat before bills ever go out. Billing attorneys review draft bills and often cut time entries that appear excessive. In other words, if it took you five hours to do a task, the billing attorney (not the associate) may change the time entry on the bill to two-and-a-half hours. Firms don't like to do this because it is potential money down the drain. But the loss of some revenue is better than the loss of a client.

Most bills include columns with the date of the work, the attorney involved, a brief description of the work, the amount of time, and the corresponding cost. Clients typically scan the cost column looking for particularly large entries and then look to see what they got for their money.

With everything else you have to learn, it may seem too much to provide detailed time entries for clients. One joke about associate time entries suggests that associates should just conclude every time entry with "and other stuff" or "and whatever." But there is a very selfish reason to communicate the benefit of your services to clients: Less of your time will get written off. Consider the following two hypothetical time entries:

Read documents; thought about case; called client	X hrs.	$750
Reviewed opposing party's pleadings for deficiencies; developed litigation strategy; telephone conference to update client and receive additional direction	X hrs.	$750

The second entry is far better at communicating the benefit of paying $750. As a result, the billing attorney is less likely to write off the time because the client is more likely to pay it without balking.

Lawyers always need to be aware of the impact of their words on others. Bills are no exception. Your time entries should not vex or perplex clients—or a billing attorney.

Tips on Time Entries

These practices will help ensure that your billable time actually ends up on a bill:

☐ **Follow client billing protocols.** Clients may have specific requirements about the format of their bills. Check with the billing attorney to see whether there are any special rules.

☐ **Tell a story.** Use your narratives to tell a story about how the work progressed and what you accomplished. For example, rather than writing "attended meeting," discuss what happened at the meeting.

☐ **When in doubt, provide more detail rather than less.** The billing attorney can always delete some of your narrative, but she probably won't know enough about what you did to supplement an insufficient narrative.

☐ **Use verbs that connote focused thought.** It is better to "participate" in a meeting than to "attend" it; it is better to "review" documents than to "look at" or "read" them; it is better to do "additional drafting" on documents than to "revise" them; and it is better to "analyze" information than to "think about" it.

☐ **Be specific.** "Research" and "revise" are fine in small doses. But if you use "research," be sure to indicate what you found and how it helps. Otherwise, it can appear that you are simply chasing rabbits down holes into oblivion—all the while generating a huge bill. "Revise" can quickly increase a client's blood pressure if it looks like a document is going back and forth between lawyers again and again with no apparent purpose. One or two sets of revisions are acceptable. After that, the client will reasonably wonder what was so wrong in the first

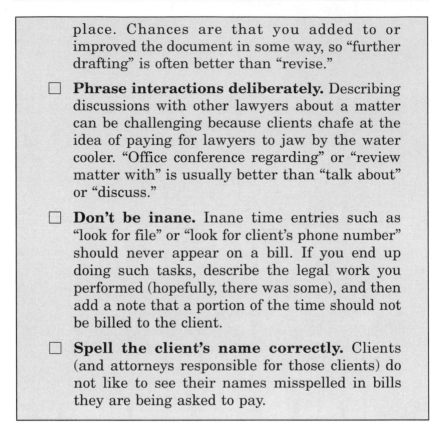

place. Chances are that you added to or improved the document in some way, so "further drafting" is often better than "revise."

☐ **Phrase interactions deliberately.** Describing discussions with other lawyers about a matter can be challenging because clients chafe at the idea of paying for lawyers to jaw by the water cooler. "Office conference regarding" or "review matter with" is usually better than "talk about" or "discuss."

☐ **Don't be inane.** Inane time entries such as "look for file" or "look for client's phone number" should never appear on a bill. If you end up doing such tasks, describe the legal work you performed (hopefully, there was some), and then add a note that a portion of the time should not be billed to the client.

☐ **Spell the client's name correctly.** Clients (and attorneys responsible for those clients) do not like to see their names misspelled in bills they are being asked to pay.

WHAT *REALLY* MATTERS: REALIZATION

Law firms that bill by the hour track all sorts of information about time and revenue. This usually includes not only billable time, but also the percentage of your billable hours that clients actually pay. This collected revenue is known as "realization" or more affectionately as "dollars in the door." The difference between the value of billable hours and dollars in the door can result from time that did not get billed or that a client did not pay.

Law firms also typically track all their costs—which include salaries of any lawyers besides those with an equity stake (partners, members, etc.). Then they divide that number by the number of lawyers in the firm to determine average overhead per lawyer. That is typically the amount of revenue you have to generate before you are deemed to "break even." But breaking even is not enough since the partners are paid only from profits—and partners are not keen on the idea of working for free.

Despite all this tracking and counting, you should not obsess about efficiency or profitability when you first join the firm. The firm will assume that if you can bill hours, it can collect them. At the outset, efficiency should be a major concern for you only if lawyers are consistently writing off more of your time than they are for other lawyers at your level (or if assigning attorneys tell you that efficiency is a problem).

As mentioned earlier, when you first start a project, you should find out about how much time the assigning lawyer thinks it should take to complete. Check in with that lawyer if it appears that coming up with an answer will take significantly longer than the estimate. But never, ever cut corners in an attempt to be "efficient." You must come up with an answer, and it must be the right answer.

Few things are more costly to a law firm than having to redo work or, worse, dispensing erroneous legal advice. Coming up with the wrong legal answer on a project is like a taxi driver who runs a red light and wrecks. The passengers don't want to pay the fare and they are angry, late, and maybe injured or worse. Clients won't pay for wrong legal advice, and if you screw up a project, other lawyers will not want to work with you in the future. No one wants to ride in a smashed-up taxi!

If you get completely bogged down on a project and do work that is not useful, the taxi driver analogy still works— you are the taxi driver who gets lost. The passengers—and clients—usually won't pay the whole bill. As a new associate, your pay will not get cut if you are inefficient. But as you progress in the firm, the amount of revenue you generate will undoubtedly affect your compensation.

Keep efficiency in the back of your mind because, ultimately, you will be judged on your "dollars in the door." But before you add that additional layer of stress to your life, work on doing the best job possible on your projects—and always meet your deadlines.

Your Dollars in the Door

Here are some reminders about keeping profitability on your radar:

☐ First and foremost, focus on doing excellent legal work and meeting deadlines.

☐ Do not cut corners in an attempt to be efficient. If you sense you need to check something, take the time to double- or triple-check. Incorrect answers are not efficient.

☐ After your first few months at the firm, ask whether your write-offs are within the firm's expectations.

☐ Understand about how much revenue you need to generate each year in order to be profitable.

PARTNER COMPENSATION

Partners care deeply about the partner compensation process, but they rarely utter a word about it to associates. That's unfortunate because knowing about the process can sometimes help to explain otherwise seemingly inexplicable behavior.

Because compensation is the "report card" at law firms, the months during which partner compensation is determined can be tense. Most of the intrigue happens out of sight of the associates, but the process can cause run-ins that associates are at a loss to explain:

A potential new client called a firm and left messages for both an associate and a partner. The associate happened to return the call first, and the partner went nuts. The associate thought he was doing the right thing by being responsive. The partner thought the associate should stay away from the partner's potential clients—even though it was only going to be a very small amount of work.

Stunned, the associate mentioned the incident to the partner who served as his mentor. The mentor smiled and chalked up the crotchety behavior to the fact that the partners were in the throes of battling it out over compensation.

As is often the case when you are a new associate, the best approach is to keep your head down—and bill.

As an associate, you are paid out of "first dollars," which means that your salary is an expense that gets paid along with other expenses of the firm. Anything left over is split among the partners. Typically, there is plenty left over, but not always. Even large, highly profitable firms have bad years in which partner compensation can dip significantly. This results in very grumpy partners.

Partner compensation is typically set by a committee and is usually based on the revenue a partner generates and the amount of business a partner controls or brings into the firm. When new work comes into a firm, it is usually assigned to an "originating" attorney and a "billing" attorney. Often those are the same attorney, but the billing attorney is the primary attorney who is responsible for the client, similar to the account executive at an advertising agency. The originating attorney may have brought a particular case to the firm because of the attorney's expertise, but may not be the primary attorney for the client. Billable hours are important for partners, but the clients they are responsible for and the amount of revenue those clients generate can be even more important.

In most firms, partners submit information to a compensation committee that highlights the partner's success at the firm in the preceding twelve months. The compensation memo, as it is sometimes called, generally includes information on new business the partner brought to the firm and the amount of revenue the firm received from the partner's clients. This includes the revenue from the work of other lawyers for the billing attorney's clients. The memo can also include any other information the lawyer deems relevant to her compensation.

One partner at a large West Coast firm was fortunate enough to have his third child just before the start of the annual compensation process. His compensation memo reportedly contained just a single sentence: "To each according to his need."

The compensation committee reviews the information and recommends compensation targets for the partners that correspond to a percentage of profits. Typically, the partners are put into several tiers. The partners in each tier receive the same percentage of profits for that year, and the percentages for each tier are progressively higher. Not surprisingly since lawyers are involved, there is often significant jockeying, cajoling—or even whining—to be put in a higher tier.

The firm's executive committee—essentially the board of directors—usually makes the final call on which partner is in which tier. Target compensation levels for the partners in each tier are determined by multiplying the firm's anticipated profits by the corresponding percentage for that tier.

Actual compensation is somewhat more complex. To help with cash flow, partners are typically paid only once a month. Their monthly draw is also less than one-twelfth of their targeted compensation. Through their monthly draws, partners may receive only a portion of their total targeted compensation. This continues until the firm has enough cash in the bank to make an extra distribution. By the end of the year, these extra distributions are supposed to bring the partners to at least their compensation target. Some firms smooth out the fluctuations in revenue collection (and hence partner compensation) by drawing on a line of credit, but at some point revenue and partner compensation have to be reconciled.

Equity partners have to buy into the partnership by making a substantial investment called a capital contribution. If the firm folds, the partners lose not only their jobs, but also their capital contribution. As a new associate who probably has lots of law school loans, you may think that having that much money to lose would be a nice problem to have. That is not what the partners think. It's their money—and they have worked very hard to earn it. Whether or not you agree with the perspective of the partners, it is useful to understand their point of view.

Financially, things aren't always as rosy for partners as you might imagine. They have to pay self-employment taxes—and the employer's portion of your taxes. They also have to pay all the business expenses of the firm before receiving a dime of compensation. Law firm partners are generally well compensated, but they also work very hard and often endure significant fluctuations in income. This helps explain why partners often think they are paid too little and that associates are paid too much.

WORKING FOR FREE

At a law firm, you are considered to be working only when your meter is on—when you are billing. You should not expect much credit for anything besides billable time. All other time—administrative time, vacation time, sick time, and sometimes even pro bono time—doesn't count as "working." In fact, most associates do not even accrue vacation or sick time. Generally, you can take vacation (or get sick) as often as you like, as long as you have met your billable-hours expectations. That often means there is not much vacation.

When you are at the office and you aren't billing, you are like the taxi driver driving around looking for a fare. You are using up firm resources, but you aren't bringing in revenue. But instead of only letting you "eat what you kill," law firms essentially advance your salary. You are expected to repay the firm—and then some—from billable work. If you don't hold up your end of the bargain, you are eating into the partners' compensation, which is not a proposition that the partners will endure indefinitely.

The fact that you don't get credit for non-billable projects doesn't mean that you don't have to do non-billable "work." But it does help explain some seemingly contradictory messages that associates may receive about their jobs. Partners may tell you to spend "all" of your time billing and then tell you that you also need to learn Continuing Legal Education material, but that you cannot bill that time.

From the partners' perspective, there is no contradiction. You are expected to bill a substantial number of hours. You also have to develop your lawyering skills on top of a full day of billing. Remember: You are essentially self-employed. A taxi driver does not get paid for the time spent maintaining his car; for all practical purposes, you do not get paid for attending CLEs, learning new areas of the law, or participating in firm administration. But these are fundamental aspects of a successful practice. Just think of your non-billable requirements as part of your firm's "working for free program."

You should also be very skeptical of any promises that you will get "credit" for non-billable work. These promises are often sincere and well meant. They can also collapse under the realities of the bottom line. Accolades and bonuses at law firms are primarily based on revenue. It is not uncommon for associates to be asked to take on large non-billable projects with the promise that the work will count toward their billable hours—only to be asked at the end of the year why their actual billable hours are low.

Being Strategic About Non-Billable Time

Here are some tips to ensure your non-billable time helps rather than harms your career:

☐ Wait a year or so before joining non-profit boards or other community organizations. Although the groups can be a great way to make a name for yourself in the community, you first need to learn to practice law.

☐ Give first priority to projects and activities that will enhance your legal skills. Working on a CLE paper for a key partner is much more beneficial than helping plan the firm picnic.

☐ Focus on non-billable work for partners with whom you want to build a relationship and lawyers who are willing to mentor you. There are plenty of lawyers who will want to shed non-billable projects just so they can spend more time billing.

☐ To avoid getting too much non-billable work, tell senior lawyers at the outset that you are soliciting work because you know you need keep up your billable hours. That way at least you will have made it clear that non-billable work will not meet your needs.

☐ You have to do your fair share of non-billable projects, but don't be a glutton for punishment. If a non-billable project will hamper your ability to do your billable work, try to decline politely—or see whether the request can be scaled back. Other lawyers won't necessarily know about your time commitments, and turning down non-billable work is likely to be deemed acceptable if you are doing large amounts of billable work.

☐ Set clear boundaries on the scope of the project. With no invoices to moderate the requests for your time, pro-bono projects in particular can mushroom from simple inquiries into massive and complex undertakings. And once you start a project, you have to see it through.

☐ Use good judgment. On occasion, there may be a huge high-profile pro bono case that can help you build your reputation and your lawyering skills. More often, huge non-billable projects will just keep you in the office on the weekends.

☐ Keep in mind that a firm may encourage pro-bono work, but generally won't believe that you are providing the firm (as opposed to society) with a great benefit if you are not also meeting your billable-hours requirements.

☐ Try to be as efficient as possible with administrative tasks—and delegate them whenever you can. When you are cleaning your desk, you are not "working."

CHAPTER 8

ENJOYING THE SWIM: MANAGING YOUR LIFE

IT'S A MARATHON—NOT A SPRINT

There actually can be too much of a good thing. Despite all the emphasis on billable hours, you should be careful about trying to be a billing superstar. As one lawyer put it, "it's a marathon—not a sprint."

You need to be honest with yourself about the pace that you can maintain over the long haul. It does not do anyone any good for you to burn out. Firms invest hundreds of thousands of dollars in associates, so there is a strong incentive for firms to want to keep you around—unless they believe the alternative is clearly better.

Unlike many jobs where the workflow process is fairly structured, at a law firm you are likely to be the only one who knows how much work you have. That means you alone have to set limits on your work. No one else is going to protect you from taking on too much work.

If you truly cannot take on another project, you must graciously say "no" or make it very clear that you cannot start it right away. (You should not say "no" to lawyers from whom you would like to get most of your work. Those lawyers may feel that they have gone out of their way to invest in you only to have you rebuff them.)

If the lawyer is not someone with whom you want to build a primary relationship, thank her for thinking of you and offer to let her know when you are available for more work. But you cannot cut corners on projects or miss deadlines. You need to have enough time for each project to complete it thoroughly and carefully. If you do a good job on projects, eventually you are likely to have more work than you can handle. If you take on too much and you blow a deadline or do sloppy work, your workload will diminish—perhaps permanently.

All of this is easier said than done, and workload management is a constant challenge even for senior lawyers. You must balance staying busy with having enough time to do excellent work on projects—and being available to do work for lawyers with whom you want to build a relationship. Over the long haul, you also need to work at a pace you can maintain.

Never canceling a vacation is a good place to set boundaries. In rare circumstances, canceling one vacation may be okay, but never two in a row. Here are one attorney's articulate thoughts on vacations and family commitments:

> If you cancel a vacation, always get a rock-solid commitment from your supervising partner for make-up time. And never, ever cancel an important family commitment without making clear to everyone involved that you are placing this *one matter* ahead of your own family because it is vitally important and you can't possibly do it to them again. If this violates your firm culture, find a different firm or plan on being single, now or later or both. This is not just a personal satisfaction issue; it is protecting the firm's investment in you. Burn-out is real; it is expensive short-term for the firm in terms of lost productivity, and it is expensive long-term in retention and replacement costs. Good management knows this. Bad management should be given the opportunity to reveal itself. The sooner you find out you've signed up with Dilbert's company, the faster you can get out and save your career and your sanity.

Putting limits on when you check your mobile device is another good place to see if you can set boundaries. Expectations about how often you must check your mobile device vary from firm to firm and even from attorney to attorney or from project to project. Check with other associates and the partners for whom you work for their expectations. If you get most of your work from a partner who expects you to be available all the time, it is worthwhile trying to get more work from other partners who do not expect you to check your mobile device constantly. If you try to set reasonable boundaries with unreasonable attorneys, they will simply think that it is you who is being unreasonable.

If you are available all the time, you set the expectation that you will be available all the time. Not being always available may mean that you miss some opportunities for work, but the work you miss is more likely to be from disorganized lawyers. There is a problem if a partner regularly cannot figure out how to delegate work until the Friday before a document is due on Monday.

When working to set boundaries, pick your battles. Some nights and weekends are part of the program. But don't surrender as a matter of course. Surrendering will ensure that you will end up in a situation that does not work for you. And you'll be sending the message that you do not stand up for yourself. On occasion, not being a team player can be seen as a sign of strength.

Finally, and most importantly, think long-term. You are in charge of your career. Consider the things that are working about your career and what needs to improve. You probably don't know what your dream job is right at first, but getting a reputation for doing excellent work will open doors to other opportunities both within and outside the firm.

Regularly take stock of your career, and make adjustments as you figure out what you want to do. This may only mean small changes in your current position, but it could mean larger, longer term changes. If you identify areas that you would like to change, put together a plan. Major changes may take a while, but try to make sure that you are always making at least incremental progress. If that means hiring a life coach, a financial planner, or a career counselor, you should seriously consider those options.

Keeping Your Career on Course

Here are some issues you should regularly consider to keep your career on track:

- ☐ Do you enjoy your work?
- ☐ Is your work rewarding?
- ☐ Do you like your colleagues?
- ☐ Does your work style fit with those of your colleagues?
- ☐ Do you like your clients?
- ☐ Are you satisfied with your compensation?
- ☐ Are you learning?
- ☐ Do you have enough time off?
- ☐ Is your work aligned with your values?
- ☐ Is there anything about your work environment that could improve?
- ☐ What are your goals for the next one, five, and ten years?
- ☐ How does your job help or hinder you from accomplishing these goals?

Getting in the habit of "documenting" your career will help you consider these questions in an organized way, and will help prepare you for job opportunities—or challenges—that may arise:

- ☐ Keep a personal file of all the presentations you have given, articles you have written, and major projects you have worked on.
- ☐ Keep copies of all your evaluations.
- ☐ Keep copies of any e-mails or other communications praising your work.
- ☐ Keep your résumé updated at least every year.

ORDER IN: WHY YOU SHOULD BUY TIME

A new lawyer arrived at the grocery store one day as a scene began to unfold on the other side of the produce section. One of the senior partners at her firm was in front of the broccoli. The associate started to go over and say hello, but stopped when she realized things were not going well. The partner had selected a generous bunch of broccoli and, with her free hand, pulled a plastic bag off the nearby roll. With the square piece of plastic in one hand and the broccoli in the other, she jabbed the broccoli toward the bag. The bag calmly fluttered aside. The partner's frustration was palpable.

Undaunted, she held the plastic square toward the light—then turned it over. She glared up at it, as if the bag had personally affronted her. Still at a loss as to how to open the bag, she shook it up and down, apparently hoping the bag would catch a downdraft and unfurl like a parachute. Still—no luck.

Here was a woman used to having things go her way. With a stern look and some carefully selected phrases, she regularly achieved minor miracles for clients. Elected officials caved when she called. But she couldn't get the broccoli into the damned bag.

The new lawyer couldn't bear to watch the scene anymore and went to shop for canned goods. The associate knew the partner had a chef at home and realized that she had not shopped in a grocery store—probably in years. She'd missed that common experience that teaches us to rub the edges of the bag together to get the two pieces of plastic to separate. As all of this unfolded, the associate became alarmed that someone could be so removed from reality. "Is this my future as a lawyer?" the associate wondered.

I had similar concerns when I learned that a partner had his car washed—at home. A service came and washed and vacuumed his car while it sat in his driveway. He was in the office working.

For me, the *coup de grâce* came when I told one of the partners I had to leave work early to pick up the mail that had been held during my recent vacation. I might as well have broken into a Gregorian chant. He had no comprehension of what I had just said. His response was simply a puzzled

"Okay," and his facial expression added: "I'll just go with this, but how is it that you *personally* have to do these things?"

The work requirements for lawyers—particularly at large law firms—are daunting. That poses major challenges for work-life balance. I once asked a highly successful partner how she maintained balance in her life with two children and a spouse who also worked at a demanding job. Her answer was simple: "I get in the office early and work a full day. I spend my evenings and weekends with my family. And someone else handles every other aspect of my life." She also exercises in the mornings and takes regular vacations.

As a new lawyer, I spent more time than I wanted cleaning house, but I was disturbed by the notion of having a housekeeper, and I was concerned that I could not afford one. I had huge debts from law school and virtually no assets. I took a baby step and started using the dry cleaning service that delivered to my office. Leave dirty clothes in a closet; two days later they are back in the same closet cleaned and ironed. I was hooked immediately. The housekeeper and grocery delivery service followed soon after.

There are many ways to "buy" free time, and you should seriously consider them. If you are so proud that you clean your own toilets, but get completely burned out or don't meet your billable-hours requirements, you are not better off. Looking at the economics may also provide some perspective. Figure out your approximate net pay per hour. Then compare that amount to the cost of hiring someone to do an hour's worth of unpleasant or time-consuming chores. Chances are, you will be way ahead if you "buy" a few hours by paying someone else to handle tasks that you do not find particularly fulfilling. The point is that lawyers are highly paid and don't have forty-hour-a-week jobs. You will probably have to "buy" free time and relaxation.

At the same time, you should not go overboard. Some lawyers quickly get used to their fancy paychecks and treat themselves with expensive vacations, cars, dinners, spa treatments—you name it. Extravagant purchases—particularly if you have loans—can cause you to have less freedom, rather than more. If you pile on even more debt soon after you graduate, you will have fewer options in the long run. If your dream job comes along at a lower salary, you may not be able to take it. And if you are laid off, additional debt only makes matters worse. In moderation, treating yourself is important. But avoid trying on the golden hand-cuffs. They can be hard to remove.

Life-Work Zen

This is your real life now. Here are some tips to maintain balance and your sanity over the long haul:

☐ Work long days and take time off. In the long run, you'll be better off working two 10.5–hour days and taking a day off instead of working three 7–hour days.

☐ Try to put some boundaries on your availability, including when you check your mobile device.

☐ Figure out what is most important in your personal life and schedule it regularly as an inviolate appointment.

☐ Take vacations. Taking vacations and other breaks from work is not selfish. Think of them as protecting the firm's investment in you. If you burn out and quit, everyone loses. So work hard, but make sure you take breaks when you need to.

☐ When you are on vacation, try to check your mobile device no more than once per day.

☐ Pay someone else to perform the time-consuming tasks that you do not enjoy, such as housecleaning or laundry.

☐ Eat out or order in.

☐ Manage stress with massages, hikes, running, meditation, yoga—whatever works for you.

☐ Multitask in your free time. Listen to the news on the treadmill or read a mindless magazine at the doctor's office.

☐ Take a creative class to use your right brain.

☐ Develop a long-term financial plan so your finances do not limit your options.

IT'S CALLED YOUR LIFE "OUTSIDE" THE OFFICE FOR A REASON

You should consider your first few months as a new lawyer as a probationary period. Particularly until you have proven yourself, you may find that some senior attorneys will be concerned by any sign that you could be distracted from your job. For the most part, it is a good idea to keep your life outside the office just that: outside the office.

The story of a new attorney who hired his firm's support staff to work on his house illustrates the point:

A new attorney had just bought a home that needed lots of work. He was busy and needed help. Fortuitously, he found that one of the messengers in the office also did carpentry on the side. The attorney hired the staff person to help with the house on weekends.

This should have been a red flag. Having any kind of special relationship with any non-attorney is generally problematic because it opens the door for other staff members to claim that one of their colleagues is getting preferential treatment. Whether or not this is true is irrelevant. The perception will exist that a non-attorney has an "in" with someone who may eventually be part of firm management.

The messenger could not do all the house projects himself, so he offered to see whether some of the other staff members from the office would also help with the work. Several agreed, and soon the attorney had a small crew from the office fixing up his house on the weekends.

Not surprisingly, the work on the house soon became part of the office chatter. To some attorneys it appeared that the associate (and the staff members) were more interested in the work on the house than the work of the firm. The attorneys mentioned "lack of focus" on the associate's review.

The gossip about the house in the office was not fatal, but it was not helpful either. In retrospect, the associate decided he should have made other arrangements for the work on the house.

For the first six months or so, you won't go wrong by focusing solely on learning to practice law. That is what senior lawyers will expect and appreciate. Once you have established yourself, you should seek out pastimes you enjoy or activities that will enhance your connections in the community, such as memberships on non-profit boards.

Still, it should never appear that your outside activities are a distraction from your work.

Don't Blur the Lines

Here are a few more tips to maintain the separation between your life inside and outside the office:

☐ If you comment on your outside activities in the office, realize that there are some attorneys who may perceive those comments as a distraction. Unless there is a reason to talk about your photography class (briefly) in the office, you may just want to take your photography class and keep it to yourself.

☐ Time is money, and lengthy stories about how you spent your weekend (unless you spent it in the office) are usually not necessary or appreciated.

☐ Treat social outings with colleagues or clients as work. Maintain your professionalism, and don't get drunk or chummy. Even if you are just socializing with new lawyers, if you do something untoward, it will get back to the office.

☐ Be careful about adding colleagues to social networking sites. It is easy to forget that potentially hundreds (or thousands) of people can see your posts on social networking sites. If you get a "friend" request from a colleague, you may want to say, "I appreciate the offer, but I make it a practice not to have colleagues as friends on this site."

☐ Even if you are selective with your contacts on social networking sites (and particularly if you are not), be circumspect about the information you post. Postings such as "I am so hung-over today"; "I hate my job"; "I work for a jerk"; and "I am feeling exploited" may well make it back to someone at your office and then spread like wildfire.

OFFICE ROMANCES: NO, NO, NO

It's late. It's dark out. You are working alone in the office with another colleague. Something clicks.

Hold your horses, cowboys and cowgirls; little good will come from an office romance. This particular path to bliss is fraught with peril.

The problem with office romances is that although they may be good for your social life, they can be bad for your career. Consider this tangled web:

A new associate began to date the receptionist. As they got more serious, he began to take her to functions for attorneys and their spouses or significant others. That meant she was the only non-attorney from the firm who attended the functions. For better or worse, law firms can be hierarchical, and having the receptionist at an "attorney-only" function rubbed some of the partners the wrong way. So be it. The associate was allowed to bring a date, and the receptionist was his date.

When the receptionist talked about the functions at the office, some staff members became jealous that she could attend these events but they could not. Perhaps one solution would have been to open the functions to everyone, but that was not in the offing.

The receptionist got to meet lots of partners at the various functions, and one of them thought she was attractive. To make things more interesting, the associate was a rising star and did most of his work for that partner.

So the associate worked on important transactions for a powerful partner and had a beautiful girlfriend, who just happened to be the receptionist. After long days at the office, she was the wind beneath his wings. Life was good for the associate, at least until the partner decided he wanted his own wind. The partner began to pay more and more attention to the receptionist. One thing led to another, and the receptionist decided to date the partner. After all, he had a bigger paycheck.

That created an uncomfortable situation for the associate. He not only lost his girlfriend, but also lost his major source of work at the firm. The partner decided the associate was competition for his love interest and did not want to have anything more to do with him. Unfair? Perhaps. Predictable? Absolutely.

Ultimately, the associate had to leave for another firm. The partner and the receptionist parted ways soon thereafter.

Perilous Waters

Here are some more cautions on office romances:

- ☐ The number one rule is to try to avoid office romances. They will complicate your life.

- ☐ Avoid dating anyone who is your supervisor, if you want to continue to work for that person. Dating a supervisor is a recipe for a sexual harassment lawsuit, and the firm will be none too pleased.

- ☐ If you start dating a supervisor, both of you should tell firm management and come up with a proposal for alternate sources of work.

- ☐ Avoid dating anyone you supervise (directly or indirectly), including any staff members. (See above, re: sexual harassment lawsuits.)

- ☐ If you do date someone in the office, maintain a professional demeanor at all times. Bedroom eyes are for the bedroom.

- ☐ You should not expect that your office romance will stay a secret. It is likely to come out, and if it does, you can expect to be the subject of relentless gossip.

- ☐ If you suspect that a colleague is involved in an office romance, stay quiet. Gossiping will not help you or them.

CHAPTER 9

TAKING THE NEXT PLUNGE: CLIENT RELATIONS

MARKETING 101: SKIP THE SCHMOOZING

A new lawyer once told me that she didn't have the first clue about how to market to clients—except to provide them with excellent service. She was wiser than she knew. At least at first, providing excellent service is just about the only thing you need to do. It is actually one of the only things you should do.

Some new lawyers seem to think that schmoozing and name-dropping are the key to success: "I had dinner with this person, drinks with that person, blah, blah, blah." No one cares. Most firms have plenty of rainmakers, and until you learn how to practice law, most firms do not want you trying to solicit business.

If you try to schmooze a senior lawyer's existing clients, you are likely to find yourself on a large yacht—wearing cement boots. If you try to schmooze anyone else, you may just look foolish. Clients won't appreciate your asking for their business when you don't have any real experience or expertise. If you provide great service and earn a good reputation, the business will come.

Here are some attributes that clients value most in their lawyers. Keep these in mind to help you provide excellent service:

Responsiveness. More than almost anything else, clients want their communications acknowledged promptly. Responding to messages promptly makes a huge positive impression on clients. Having clients in far-away time zones can make responsiveness more challenging. They may be waiting for an answer while you are sleeping. And mobile devices have raised clients' expectations about responsiveness. But when you don't respond promptly to a client's voicemail or e-mail, the message you send the client is: "I have more important things to do than to deal with you and your problems." When clients get that message, they often take their problems elsewhere. Responsiveness does not mean you have to give instant answers to complex questions; it *does* mean you need to let the clients know that their problems are a top priority. Respond to calls and client e-mails *at least* the same day (or have your assistant check in if you absolutely cannot). Then keep clients updated regularly so that they don't have to call you.

Timeliness. Meeting deadlines is critical with legal work. In many cases, a missed deadline can constitute malpractice. But even when a deadline is not critical, lengthy delays make clients grumpy. They often cannot proceed with some aspect of their business until their legal issues are resolved. You need to provide useful information to the client as soon as possible. That may mean breaking down a project into smaller parts and finding out what the client needs to know immediately and what can wait a little longer. When estimating your completion date, always build in time for another lawyer to review your work—and other contingencies. The minute you promise to have something done the next day, an absolute emergency will come up and consume the rest of that time.

Useful legal advice. You need to understand what the client is trying to accomplish—or avoid—so that you give advice that promotes the client's business needs to the greatest extent possible. If an action the client is proposing to take poses legal risks, you should work to find an alternative with fewer legal risks. Simply telling a client that a course of action is prohibited will not be well received, unless you have demonstrated that you have done your best to come up with other workable approaches that achieve the client's goals. Likewise, you need to make sure you give clients complete answers or make it clear that the answers are limited in scope. If a client asks whether an action is legal under state law, the client is probably assuming that only state law applies. If you just tell the client "yes," the action is legal under state law, and it turns out the action is prohibited under federal law, you are likely to have a frustrated client.

Absolutely accurate legal advice. Your advice must be absolutely accurate. Clients often rank this attribute lower than the three above because clients simply assume (and expect) that they will get accurate legal advice.

Intelligence. Clients will also assume that you are smart. Try not to do anything to suggest otherwise. You will help yourself in that respect by making sure you know the person or entities that you represent, and if there is more than one, exactly how they are related. You should also gather your thoughts before you talk to a client so that you can give concise, coherent answers, and won't have to call back and say, "oh, just one more thing." Finally, do not give advice on the fly. A client may blindside you by calling you out of the blue from a meeting, ask a complex legal question, and put you on speakerphone so that you can give the answer to everyone in the room. Resist the pressure to give an answer on the spot—you could easily be wrong in front of a lot of people. Instead, use the time to confirm the relevant facts, and then say something along the lines of, "I understand the issue, and I need to check on a few things and get back to you." This tells the client that you are careful and that legal issues are not conducive to instant answers.

Someone who cares. One of the most important services you provide to clients is demonstrating that you are an ally ready to help them through a complex—and often harrowing—situation. Clients may need to vent about their legal problems. Within reason, let them. If clients could deal with a situation themselves, they wouldn't need a lawyer.

Friendship. If clients enjoy working with you, the whole process is more enjoyable for everyone. Such simple human behavior as a little humor in the midst of a stressful situation or remembering a client's birthday will go a long way toward building goodwill. After a project ends, keep in touch by sending notes about new legal developments.

TAKE A SEAT ON THE COUCH: THE IMPORTANCE OF EMPATHIZING

Sometimes being a lawyer can be a lot like being a therapist. A huge part of the job is listening. You need to let clients know that you hear them and that you are a capable ally in helping them solve their problem.

Clients may have legal problems because they have done something monumentally stupid. It can be easy to roll your eyes. But the last thing clients need is for you to judge them. When you interact with clients, you need to make it clear that you are an unfailing ally and that your unwavering focus is to resolve their problem—no matter how it came about. It may help to remember that unless clients had legal problems, lawyers would not have jobs.

Legal issues almost always involve some stress for the client—even when the client has not screwed up. There is the gamesmanship of contract negotiations, the stress of a make-or-break lawsuit, or the emotions of a messy divorce. Legal fees just add to the stress.

Even as a new lawyer, the concepts of rules and legal commitments, and of courts to enforce those rules and commitments, are second nature. For clients, the law can be a minefield of unknown dangers. As a lawyer, you can add to your client's stress by having to deliver bad news. That news can have dramatic negative consequences for your client.

Thus, clients may need to vent—and you need to let them. They often need to do that before they can work with you rationally to make the most of a difficult situation. You may find that clients express their frustration about things they can do nothing about—that's often *why* they are venting. To lawyers, that can seem futile—if not childish. Clients can grouse that they wish the sky were yellow; that won't make it so. But if you don't listen to the client's frustration about legal issues—who will? Showing empathy in these situations will help you build trust with your client that you have heard her and that you are on the same side—despite the fact that you may have to tell her something she does not want to hear. The client will appreciate your frankness—along with your patience.

Listening to what moves your clients will also help you learn more about your client's needs, and that will help you to learn to address emotionally charged situations with circumspection. A critical skill for lawyers is to learn to diffuse tension and find the most logical pathway to meet your client's needs. You can't provide very useful advice unless you understand the client's needs.

There are a few caveats about all this: Listening carefully to clients and being empathetic about their legal concerns does not mean that you should let clients dump on you about personal problems (unless perhaps you are a divorce attorney)—or that you should not bill clients for listening. You also should not have to put up with rudeness or abuse from clients. If that happens, respectfully call the client on the behavior or talk to the attorney who is in charge of the client.

Showing Clients More Care

Lawyers can't live without clients. Here are some tips for building long-lasting relationships:

☐ Make it clear to clients that you will be their unfailing ally.

☐ Take the initiative to learn about the client's business and legal needs.

☐ Regularly thank clients (and for that matter other lawyers in the firm) for allowing you to work with them.

☐ Be friendly and available.

☐ Show clients that their work is important by being responsive and keeping them informed—even if just to say the work is still progressing.

☐ Do not tell clients that you have been delayed in working on their project because you had to do work for another client. That sends only one message: "You are less important."

☐ Focus carefully on your client's specific problem rather than providing general legal recitations. Clients usually don't care about someone else's case unless it directly affects their situation.

☐ Stay in touch with clients after a matter concludes.

"EVERYTHING I NEEDED TO KNOW ABOUT PRACTICING LAW, I LEARNED WAITING TABLES"

An attorney once remarked to me: "The job that best prepared me for being a lawyer was my job as a waiter." It made sense when he explained that being a waiter helped him learn to anticipate client needs.

If you only react to client requests, you are like a waiter who only refills a glass when the guest with a parched throat flags him down. That's not optimal client service. The importance of anticipating client needs doesn't mean that you should go off and do lots of legal work that the client never requested. That and the accompanying bill will get you in trouble quickly. But you should learn as much as you can about clients and their issues, and regularly ask yourself, "What else could I do that would help the client?"

It's not a competition to come up with the most ideas. When you first start practicing law, you won't know enough about a client—or the law—to come up with brilliant new ideas daily. That's not the point. Just get in the habit of asking yourself, "What else could I do to help the client," and pass those ideas on to the senior lawyer. Just taking the initiative to think beyond a discrete project will earn you points.

Do not contact the client directly with your ideas, though. Always check with the senior lawyer. Your idea may not be workable—or may be wrong—and checking in can keep you from appearing uninformed.

Lawyers are also protective of their clients, and many won't want to see you building independent relationships with their clients—at least until they are comfortable with how you interact with clients. Your first job is to build relationships with other *lawyers*. You don't do that by making them feel threatened. But if another lawyer takes your idea and passes it on to a client, you are well on your way to making yourself indispensable to that lawyer. At least at first, you don't need to worry about taking credit; you need to worry about making other lawyers look smart.

Anticipate Client Needs

How can you anticipate what a client may need? Here are a few ideas:

☐ Ask other lawyers how your project fits into the client's larger goals.

☐ Listen carefully. Making a client feel heard is critical to building client relationships.

☐ Make sure that whatever advice you give addresses the client's needs—and keep in mind that the client may not be asking the right question.

☐ Be curious about your clients and the work of the other lawyers in the office.

☐ Keep up on new developments in the law that may affect your client.

HELPING CLIENTS CHOOSE THEIR BATTLES

My first lesson in client service came via speakerphone. I was brand new at the firm, and my modest office was next door to the cavernous corner office of a senior partner. He had a habit of keeping his door open and counseling clients in a thunderous voice on the speakerphone. He could do what he wanted. But for a merger, his name would still have been on the wall in the lobby.

A divorce client had called. She had changed her mind and wanted the refrigerator.

"Well, I'll tell you what," the partner boomed. "I can probably get that refrigerator for you. But you should think about this. It will probably cost you a lot more than the refrigerator is worth. You are getting out of a marriage you hate, you are getting a good settlement, and you don't have any venereal diseases, so you may want to forget the refrigerator."

There was a stunned pause on the other end of the line. It became uncomfortably long. The partner's secretary who sat right outside my office shot me a look that said, "You didn't hear any of this—and if you did, we have to kill you."

Stammering, the client finally said, "Yes, okay, uh—you are right. Forget the refrigerator," and promptly hung up.

I learned then that clients caught up in the heat of a dispute are not always inclined to act in their own best interest. It is the lawyer's job to lay out the pros and cons devoid of the emotion that often clouds judgment. Clients may savor the idea of using lawyers to exact revenge on adversaries. But that kind of revenge costs hundreds of dollars an hour, and if revenge is the primary goal, the aftertaste for clients is often bitter.

As long as a claim is not frivolous, it is entirely the client's decision whether to pursue it. And you need to make it clear that if a client decides to proceed with a matter, you will pursue it vigorously. But you must inform the client of the risks and potential rewards of proceeding. Clients may also ask you if you think it is okay for them to do something that is perfectly legal—and monumentally stupid. Clients are always in the best position to make judgments about their business. But studies have shown that of all business advisors, executives consider lawyers to be among the most vital. So it is not enough simply to tell a client that a course of action is legal—if a lawsuit or some other mess is also likely to occur. You need to tell the client that the course of action will probably result in a lawsuit—even if it is one the client would almost never lose.

At the same time, you can't substitute your judgment for the client's. There are always considerations other than legal (such as financial or operational) that play into a decision about pursing a lawsuit or a business transaction. So you should refrain from getting involved in the business aspects of a deal—unless those decisions could have legal impacts (for example, the transaction appears so unfavorable to a client that it might result in a shareholder lawsuit). It is fine to tell clients the terms of similar transactions or that the client might be able to get a better price, but it is not appropriate to tell her that you don't think she's getting a good deal. That is the client's decision—and one you are not qualified to make.

If a client does insist on a course of action that seems unreasonable, you should gently confirm that decision in writing, along with the information you provided about potential outcomes. Clients who end up with unfavorable outcomes and large bills sometimes want someone else to blame, and the lawyer is an obvious target.

Helping Clients Gain Perspective

The decisions are the client's, but those decisions should be based on your sound advice:

☐ Clients who are fed up with an adversary are often eager to use litigation to inflict pain, and you need to make sure your client understands that litigation almost always involves many risks and costs lots of money.

☐ You must make it clear that your client ultimately decides whether to pursue a matter, but you must also make your client aware of the risks and rewards, while reassuring him that if he does pursue the matter, you will represent his interests vigorously.

☐ When you communicate risks to your client, be sure to put them in writing and to keep a record.

THE CRITICAL IMPORTANCE OF CONFIDENTIALITY

The importance of maintaining the confidentiality of attorney-client communications is one of the very underpinnings of our legal system. The ability and duty of lawyers to maintain client confidences is often one of the key reasons that clients seek advice from attorneys. You must take great care not to reveal confidential client information. Blabbing about client information is one of the quickest ways to lose the trust of clients and other lawyers, or potentially even find yourself on the other side of a bar complaint.

Keep Your Jaw Shut

Here are some important reminders about confidential client information:

☐ Be careful about conversations in public places such as restaurants and elevators. The person behind you in the elevator might work for opposing counsel, the opposing party, or someone else who should not hear about your work. A third party overhearing a conversation could compromise the attorney-client privilege.

☐ If you must discuss client business in public places, refrain from using names or other facts that would enable someone overhearing the conversation to connect it with the legal matter involved.

☐ Exercise caution with cell phone conversations. Ask to call the client back if you cannot talk privately.

☐ Refrain from discussing one client's business with another client. If clients think you are speaking indiscriminately about another client's business, they will assume that you do the same about their business.

☐ Be careful about discussing the specifics of your work even with family members. One attorney recounted this story: At a private social gathering, a client's spouse mentioned something highly confidential, but quite interesting, to the attorney's spouse, only to have the attorney's wife respond with an "I don't know what you are talking about" look and comment. The client later told the attorney that he was extremely impressed and appreciative of the attorney's discretion.

☐ Don't gossip at your client's expense. It is not worth violating the ethics rules to entertain your friends with juicy confidences that you learned at the office. You will be betraying your

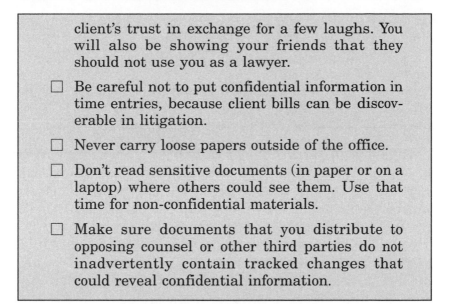

client's trust in exchange for a few laughs. You will also be showing your friends that they should not use you as a lawyer.

☐ Be careful not to put confidential information in time entries, because client bills can be discoverable in litigation.

☐ Never carry loose papers outside of the office.

☐ Don't read sensitive documents (in paper or on a laptop) where others could see them. Use that time for non-confidential materials.

☐ Make sure documents that you distribute to opposing counsel or other third parties do not inadvertently contain tracked changes that could reveal confidential information.

NEVER FORGET: CYA

As if you did not have enough to pay attention to, you also need to make sure you document key milestones and communications on projects.

In a more dignified era, lawyers rarely sued other lawyers. Today, entire firms are devoted to suing other lawyers. When clients don't get the result they want, they may look for someone to blame. A law firm with a large malpractice policy is an easy target. Law firms may settle even frivolous claims just to avoid bad publicity.

To protect the firm (and your reputation), you must be able to demonstrate—even long after the fact—the essentials of what you were asked to do and what you did. It is also important to document what you did *not* do. "Buyer's remorse" can cause a client's memories about a situation to change. After a client has paid a settlement and a nasty lawsuit has gone away, the client may decide that the settlement wasn't such a good idea. With the threat of the lawsuit gone, the client decides it could have won the lawsuit and sues the law firm for the cost of the settlement—and legal fees. The firm needs to be able to show that the client made the decision to settle based on a complete understanding of the potential risks.

You need to be particularly vigilant about documentation in certain circumstances. One of those is when there might otherwise be some ambiguity about whether a party is a client. Whether or not a party is a client dramatically changes your obligations with respect to that party.

Thus, communications with potential or former clients warrant special attention. You and the potential (or former) client may have vastly different expectations. If a former client asks for legal advice and, for whatever reason, the firm chooses not to reengage the client (firm now has a conflict, client was a jerk, etc.), the fact that the firm will not represent the former client must be clearly documented so that if the former client later runs into legal problems, the former client cannot blame you for sitting on the sidelines. These same cautions hold true for potential clients who may think that just by calling you, you become their lawyer.

Another situation in which it is particularly important to document your communication involves client conduct that is likely to be illegal. Consider the client who calls to complain about the high cost of disposing of dry cleaning chemicals and then asks what might happen if the chemicals "accidentally spilled" down the storm drain instead. The client may be thinking large fines if it gets caught; you tell the client that the potential consequences even include jail time.

That is a communication you must document. A few days of eating dry meatloaf and canned green beans in the pokey could make any client "forget" that you warned against the dumping and informed the client of the consequences. To stay out of the pokey yourself, you need to be able to document that you did not assist the client in any way in undertaking an illegal activity. And clients (and juries in malpractice cases) generally expect lawyers to confirm any extremely important advice in writing.

The need for documentation is not limited to external communications. It is also critical to retain a record of the essential aspects of your work—and to proactively document important communications both to clients and to other lawyers in your firm. If blame is being spread around, you must be able to show that you acted reasonably and responsibly. Pay particular attention to documenting communications with disorganized clients or lawyers. If the firm blows a deadline because your document sat on a partner's desk, your numerous written reminders to the partner should help keep you from having to take the fall.

Much of the information that you need to document can be included in any written work product that you prepare for an assignment. The firm also needs to retain a record that the client actually received your advice. This can be an e-mail, a transmittal letter, or some other means, but all your documentation may be of little value if you cannot show that you sent it to the client.

Some issues warrant separate written communication, such as your knowledge of any course of action the client may be contemplating that is particularly risky (or outright illegal). When in doubt, talk to a senior lawyer about whether to send a separate communication on a particular issue to a client.

Document, Document, Document

Keeping a coherent record of what occurred on a project can be particularly challenging with the barrage of information that originates from meetings, faxes, e-mails, and phone calls. Your assistant—or other lawyers in the firm—should be able to help you set up a system. Despite the challenges, it is essential to document and retain at least the following:

☐ When you received an assignment

☐ When you provided documents to assigning lawyers, to clients, or to opposing counsel

☐ Any deadlines

☐ When you completed an assignment

☐ A concise statement of your assignment

☐ The crux of the legal advice you provided

☐ The legal authorities that you researched as part of the assignment

☐ Any significant issues that were expressly beyond the scope of the assignment (and you therefore did not address)

☐ Any risks or potential consequences that you identified

☐ Any client actions you know about that are contrary to your advice—or could otherwise create legal liability

☐ Any time the firm declines to take on a client

CHAPTER 10

OTHER FISH IN THE SEA: OPPOSING COUNSEL AND THE MEDIA

WORKING WITH OPPOSING COUNSEL

Learning to work with opposing counsel takes practice. You need to be assertive, but not obnoxious, and respectful, but not fawning. It is also critical to think strategically:

As an associate headed out to a meeting with opposing counsel with the goal of reaching a settlement, the managing partner asked, "So what are you going to tell opposing counsel?" The associate replied that he was going to tell opposing counsel that he had exhaustively researched the law and that the law clearly supported the firm's client, so the other party should settle.

"No," the managing partner boomed, "You are going to tell opposing counsel that our client is best friends with the firm's managing partner and will never settle." The case settled promptly thereafter—exactly the result the client wanted.

You need to remember that despite your best efforts, opposing counsel is not going to agree with your legal positions. Senior lawyers representing opposing parties may also try to get away with things they would not try with more senior lawyers. As the associate in this story learned, it is important to prepare carefully and then stand your ground:

The brand-new associate was on the phone with opposing counsel. The associate's client was about to get sued. Opposing counsel had many, many years of experience and was not in the mood to dither. "You all can't do that," opposing counsel said definitively. "My client even wrote the law."

The associate had read the statute and the regulations over and over. The associate thought the law supported his client's position and stood his ground. He calmly explained his interpretation of the statute. Opposing counsel would have nothing to do with it. "I'm sorry, you just don't know what you are talking about," the opposing counsel quipped.

Realizing that opposing counsel would not agree, or even listen to logic, the new associate simply said, "Well, that is our position."

The associate's client did get sued and won on the very point the associate had discussed with opposing counsel.

Rules of Engagement

Here are some reminders about working with opposing lawyers:

☐ **Be firm, but respectful.** Practicing law is difficult enough without incivility. Being a jerk is not in your client's best interests. It usually only makes the other side more stubborn. You might also end up seeking a job or a referral from opposing counsel some day.

☐ **Use preparation to your advantage.** Know the law cold. It is unlikely that a senior lawyer has had time to look at the applicable law as closely as you have.

☐ **Stand your ground.** Check with a senior lawyer in your firm about your conclusions, and then stand your ground. Realize that opposing counsel can never admit that your position is correct (although you can be sure that opposing counsel will evaluate your analysis and communicate the risks to her client).

☐ **Think strategically.** Know how the law applies to your client's situation, but also ferret out any other leverage your client may have over the other party. For example, the other party might not be able to close on an important transaction, if your client files a lawsuit. These are the kinds of things you must know.

☐ **Tell the truth.** Any short-term gain that you may achieve for your client by shaving the truth is not worth the damage to your reputation. And any gain is likely to unravel as soon as the truth comes out.

☐ **Don't take things personally.** If opposing counsel is being a jerk, it probably just means that you are doing your job. It also might mean that opposing counsel is just a jerk. Either way, you should not take it personally.

☐ **Do not take abuse or allow yourself to be bullied.** Remember that no one can make you say "yes" when you want to say "no." If opposing counsel is being obnoxious, do your best to maintain your composure, and then say something along the lines of: "We don't seem to be getting anywhere, so we should discuss this another time."

☐ **Fall back on the client.** If you are feeling pushed on a particular point, you can always say, "I will need to check with my client." That should end the discussion.

HANDLING MEDIA INQUIRIES

Because of confidentiality issues, neither your client nor your firm is likely to want you to speak with reporters. And even if there is a reason to speak to the press, the firm is likely to want only one spokesperson on an issue to help prevent reporters from digging up inconsistencies. That spokesperson is likely to be from management of the firm or the client.

Thus, it is unlikely that you will be allowed to speak to reporters, but particularly if you work on high-profile matters, reporters may call. Here are some tips:

☐ If a reporter calls, find out the reporter's deadline and tell the reporter that you need to check to see whether there is any information that you can provide. Pass the request along to firm management and then respond accordingly.

☐ If you are tempted to give a reporter an anonymous tip or to speak off the record, remember that reporters can make mistakes. A reporter could inadvertently attribute information to you by name when you thought the attribution would read, "according to sources close to the transaction." That could be difficult to explain to the client and the firm.

☐ If you know that you cannot speak to the media about a particular matter (which is likely to be the case), simply say something along the lines of, "I am sorry, but we cannot litigate or negotiate in the press." That sounds better than, "I can't comment."

☐ If you are authorized to communicate with reporters, providing written answers (approved by the client) to written questions will help prevent misunderstandings and subsequent mistakes in the press.

CHAPTER 11

SWIMMING LIKE A PRO: LEGAL SKILLS IN THE REAL WORLD

CONTRACT DRAFTING: THINK WIN–WIN

As you progress in your career, depending on your area of practice, you are likely to be given responsibility for contract negotiations and drafting or handling discrete aspects of litigation, such as taking depositions. Both types of skills will help you develop as a lawyer.

With contract drafting, one of the hardest things for many new lawyers to learn is that the other side needs to win. Not everything, mind you. Not even most things. But there is a lot of truth to the saying that you have a good contract when neither side feels like it got what it wanted. Parties typically enter into a contract to define a long-term relationship. If that relationship is not mutually beneficial, it often unravels.

New associates are typically overzealous in trying to fight tooth and nail for even the most inconsequential contract terms. The zeal is admirable, but can lead to a deal that collapses—either before it ever comes together or soon thereafter. Lawyers can sometimes draft airtight contracts, and sometimes they can even force the other side to perform. But clients usually do not have the time, money, or inclination to go to court to enforce each and every provision of a contract against an intractable contractor. If one party comes out of contract negotiations embittered and demoralized, that party is not going to be a good partner for your client.

As with most legal matters, in drafting a contract you first need to identify your client's primary goals—particularly the "deal-breakers," without which it does not make sense for your client to proceed with the transaction. A client's goals for the transaction may be fairly nebulous at the outset (for example, "as much money as possible"), so it is helpful to work with the client to define and refine the "must-haves" and the "nice-to-haves" early on.

After you have identified the best-possible outcomes for your client, you can prepare for the worst-case scenarios. Try to identify the most likely negative circumstances that could arise over the term of the contract and then try to imagine the most devastating circumstances that could arise. In divining the latter, a dose of paranoia can be extremely helpful. Then figure out how to protect your client from the worst-case scenarios as well as the more likely, less serious outcomes. Regardless of the negative consequences that might arise in the future, you need to have developed a strategy to make sure your client can come out relatively unscathed.

When you come up with approaches to address the potential negative consequences, then it is time to figure out what you can give the other side with the least detriment to your client.

It is important to focus on what motivates the other party. If you know what the other party needs, you are better able to address those needs in ways that do not negatively impact your client. Often, pure profit is not at the top of the list for the other party. There may be many ways to meet the other party's needs—some of which are more palatable to your client than others. By focusing on the other party's needs and not just its stated demands, you can often identify solutions to issues that meet both parties' needs. At the very least, you may be able to find things to "give away" to the other side without compromising your client's primary objectives.

Despite all this, actually meeting your client's objectives through negotiations can be challenging, and clients may want to defer decisions on tough issues to a future contract amendment or a separate agreement. Generally, that is not advisable. Thorny issues rarely disappear. Agreements to reach agreement in the future are usually unenforceable, and often just delay discussions to a time when your client has less leverage. If your client insists on putting off decisions on key provisions, include a decision-making mechanism in the contract (such as arbitration). If the parties do not agree to critical provisions or provide a mechanism for determining them, you may not have created an enforceable contract.

Finally, negotiations can get intense and even testy. If opposing counsel is misbehaving, it is probably just a sign that you are doing your job well. Try to keep the discussions on track. Bad behavior is almost always counterproductive and generally just causes the other party to become less flexible. If negotiations get so heated that they are unproductive or harmful to your client, stay calm and insist on taking a break or rescheduling the discussions.

SMART NEGOTIATIONS

These tips will help you achieve your client's objectives in negotiations:

☐ Give the most attention to your client's most critical issues. Some new lawyers are such sticklers about each and every single point that they come close to killing the deal. If you push on every little issue, you open the door for the opposing party to give in on many of those small issues and then argue that it has been flexible.

☐ Figure out the worst possible negative consequences that could happen under the contract, and make sure your client is protected.

☐ Figure out the most likely negative occurrences that could happen under the contract, and make sure your client is protected.

☐ Discourage your client from deferring decisions on key issues.

☐ Avoid the other party's forms. Your client may want to use the other party's forms as a starting point for negotiations in order to try to save money or to be accommodating. This is usually a very bad idea. It usually takes far longer to negotiate away from lopsided provisions than it does to start from scratch.

☐ Understand the practical impacts of every provision in the document. For example, indemnification provisions are not worth much if the opposing party has no assets or insurance. Similarly, a promise to pay attorneys' fees from a party without assets is an empty promise.

☐ Research other deals involving the opposing party. If a party has given another entity the same thing that your client is asking for, it will be hard to deny it to your client.

☐ Don't start out with your client's bottom line. Propose key provisions that are aggressive but reasonable so that you have room to move in negotiations.

☐ Put a lid on new issues. To limit the proliferation of new issues late in the negotiations, it may be helpful to suggest that your client will not consider new issues unless your client receives something in exchange. (Check with your client about this, of course.)

☐ Be respectful. You will likely have to work with the opposing lawyers in the future, and your client is proposing to enter into an ongoing relationship with the other party.

☐ Do not escalate bad behavior. If opposing counsel is a jerk, it is likely a sign that you are representing your client's interests well. Don't take abuse, but try to stay focused on your client's objectives.

☐ Always keep in mind that your client must make the ultimate call on the business deal. When you talk to the other side's lawyer, you can say that you believe certain provisions may be workable or reasonable, but you must check with your client before you can represent that they are acceptable.

☐ If you send out documents to opposing counsel that your client has not reviewed, make it clear that the documents are subject to change.

☐ Once you have agreed upon a provision, document the agreement and do not propose to change it again—unless the provision is clearly problematic. Little is more frustrating than working to reach agreement only to have one party renege just before the document is signed. If you propose to make changes to provisions that are already settled upon, you are likely to get an earful from opposing counsel. Likewise, do not allow any backsliding from the other side.

☐ Use defined terms consistently. Identifying the same thing with many slightly different phrases is crazy-making for other lawyers and likely to lead to disputes. You should define terms that appear repeatedly in your document, and use only the defined term. If "Ecology" means the "State Department of Ecology," then "Ecology Department," "Department of Ecology," "SDE," and "State Ecology Department" will just inject ambiguity into your contract.

☐ Be crystal clear with your language. Any ambiguity creates the potential for a dispute. Make sure each provision of your contract can mean only what you intend. Use examples, formulas, or whatever else you need to illustrate the exact meaning. Vagueness is appropriate only on rare occasions, such as when describing your own client's obligations.

☐ Maintain document control. Try to do all the agreed-upon drafting so that new issues do not crop up every time you get a document back from opposing counsel.

☐ If the other party does any drafting, insist that all changes be identified in a redline.

☐ Verify the changes that are made to the document to ensure they were the changes you agreed upon.

☐ Write neatly when you make handwritten edits to a document to minimize word-processing errors.

RAISE YOUR RIGHT HAND: TAKING YOUR FIRST DEPOSITION

Taking your first deposition is likely to be much less daunting than you expect. A lawyer once commented to me that "nothing very good can happen to the witness whose deposition is being taken." The fact that little good can happen to a witness at a deposition also means that little bad can happen to the lawyer taking the deposition. That should be some comfort to the new lawyer sitting in the conference room for the first time with the court reporter, witness, and opposing counsel.

The usual purposes of a deposition are to gather evidence that a party can use to support its case and to "lock in" a witness's testimony. If the lawyer comes out of a deposition with any evidence, the lawyer is in better shape than when she went in. The typical goals for most witnesses are to say as little as possible that is damaging and to leave openings to supplement their answers later on.

Preparation is the best antidote for anxiety and will help ensure that the deposition is as productive as possible. Research your case thoroughly so that you know what information you need to try to get from the deposition. Once you know the evidence you need to support your legal arguments, preparation is simply a matter of coming up with questions to get that information from the witness.

Even as a new lawyer, you are likely to be much more familiar with the process—and therefore much more confident—than the witness. The rules are also on your side. A deposition is one of the few times that the opposing lawyer can say almost nothing. The opposing lawyer can make some limited objections, but the witness generally has to answer anyway (unless the question involves privileged information). Otherwise, the defending lawyer generally has to keep quiet.

It is helpful to remember that a deposition is also only one way of getting information. It is likely that you have much of the information you need from interrogatories or requests for admission. In many ways, a deposition is icing on the cake. (If the witness were truly critical to the case, a more senior lawyer would be taking the deposition.) As with many aspects of practicing law, you should prepare, focus, and relax. In the unlikely event that something does go awry, you can always ask for a break and contact a colleague.

Deposition Goals

Generally, all depositions share a few main goals:

- ☐ Putting the witness at ease so that the witness will be talkative

- ☐ Gaining a better understanding of the role of the various players involved

- ☐ Gaining a better understanding of the facts of the case

- ☐ Obtaining specific evidence to support your theory of the case

- ☐ Authenticating documents

Reading through the transcript of the first half-hour of most depositions is extremely tedious. First, the court reporter swears in the witness, and then the lawyer typically launches into an extremely detailed inquiry into the witness's background—often starting in high school or even before. Much of the information is irrelevant: The primary goal is to put the witness at ease and get the witness used to answering questions. The lawyer is "lubricating" the witness.

A detailed outline can make taking a deposition almost foolproof. It will serve as a checklist to ensure you don't forget to ask a critical question. Just having an outline should help allay your anxiety. If you have a very detailed outline, taking the deposition primarily involves just methodically going through your questions. The court reporter or videographer records the answers. But you should still listen carefully to the answers in case something surprising or unexpected arises. You should also note critical questions that the witness does not answer the way you wanted. Later in the deposition, you may be able to ask the question a different way to get the information you need.

Here is a suggested format for a deposition outline. Everyone has a different style, so modify your outline so that it works for you, but include at least the following:

- ☐ Start with a warm introduction to try to put the witness at ease.

- ☐ Tell the witness the general rules about depositions (answering verbally, speaking so the court reporter can hear, looking into the camera, etc.).

- ☐ Ask the witness to state his or her name and address for the record.

- ☐ Ask about the witness's background.

- ☐ Ask about other individuals involved and their roles.

- ☐ Ask about the witness's role.

- ☐ Ask the witness to authenticate documents for use as exhibits (identify the document, the person who signed it, etc.).

- ☐ Ask any other questions you need to get information to support your key legal arguments.

Deposition Tips

Here are a few more tips to help you prepare for your depositions:

☐ Sit in on other depositions.

☐ Read other deposition transcripts to familiarize yourself with the process, paying attention to how the questions were asked and answered.

☐ Use a checklist or other system to keep track of what information you have obtained in the deposition and what information you still need.

☐ Keep your questions short and direct.

☐ Ask summarizing questions (paraphrasing prior answers) to clarify key information.

☐ Lead up to critical questions in small steps—or drop them in the middle of mundane questions when the witness is off guard.

☐ Try not to let the witness leave an opening to add or clarify testimony at a later time. Use such follow-up questions as "Anything else?" or "Is that everything?" to find out whether there is any additional information the witness can provide.

☐ Do not follow your outline slavishly. Pay attention to the witness's answers, and if there are areas that warrant additional probing, probe away. Above all, as a lawyer you are paid to think.

☐ Before you dismiss a witness, ask to take a break and then use that time to double-check your list. Make sure you have asked everything you wanted to ask and that you don't need to follow up or clarify any answers. You should assume that you will not be able to depose the witness again.

CHAPTER 12

SWIMMING AWAY

_____

LEAVING WITHOUT MAKING WAVES

It may seem ironic to have a chapter on leaving your job in a book about how to succeed at your job. Ideally, you should stay at your first job at least a year. Any less and you may look like a job-hopper, particularly if your next job doesn't work out. Besides, it usually takes at least a year to figure out whether you can make a job work for you.

But there are rare occasions when the perfect offer comes along shortly after you have taken another job—or you can tell fairly quickly that your prince of a job actually has lots and lots of warts. Unless you get an offer for your dream job, you should first try to make things work with your existing employer.

If you end up assigned to an incorrigible partner, try to extricate yourself from the partner but stay with the firm. Particularly in large firms, the experience of associates varies widely since large firms are really just a conglomeration of practice groups sharing a single logo. The culture of different groups can vary dramatically.

It is also risky to leave a job before you have another one. No matter what you say, some interviewers will think that you were either forced to leave—or that you are disloyal. You don't need those strikes against you at the outset.

Most important, when it does come time to leave, you must not burn your bridges. That is not the time to unburden your soul, "fix" the firm, or exact revenge. If you do, you are the one who will ultimately lose the most.

A first-year associate who was very friendly and easygoing did end up with a great job offer at a different firm. The new job gave her a better opportunity to practice the kind of law she wanted, and the job was much closer to her home. She announced that she was leaving and gave those reasons. The firm went into action to try to keep her. A senior partner asked to meet with her and pressed her on her reasons for leaving. Finally, the associate admitted that she was also leaving because the firm appeared to be having financial difficulties. She then proceeded to provide suggestions on the way the firm could improve operations.

The conversation went rapidly downhill. The partner told her she did not know what she was talking about and that he thought she had better judgment. This was the partner who moments before was trying to get her to stay at the firm.

The normally jovial and unflappable associate was dismayed. The conversation had not gone as expected. She had been asked for all of the reasons she was leaving, and she had tried to be helpful. In return, she got blasted.

This associate's experience is not unusual. Firms don't like to lose valued associates, particularly to competitors. Partners have a lot of their money invested in associates and significant pride invested in the firm. Departures also put other lawyers in the sometimes uncomfortable position of thinking about their own choices and futures.

Whenever associates announce that they are planning to leave, firms almost always try very hard to talk them out of their decision. The conversation usually does not involve changing work requirements or perks because those are generally standardized for associates. Instead, the conversation usually focuses on future opportunity: "You have more growth potential here because we are a large firm (or a small firm)," etc. Generally, you should take the entreaties with a grain of salt. If the efforts at retaining the associate fail, hard feelings often ensue—not unlike a divorce.

Ultimately, little good can come of providing "suggestions" to change the firm after you have announced your departure. No captain of a ship would appreciate having an inexperienced crew member first jump into a lifeboat and then shout back that the ship was sinking.

TIPS FOR LEAVING

Here are some tips for leaving with grace:

☐ **Do not say anything about leaving until you have definitely decided to do so.**

☐ **Consider the order in which you notify your colleagues.** The news may spread like wildfire, and you don't want the managing partner to hear the news from her assistant. An appropriate order may be: first, the senior lawyers with whom you work most closely, and second, firm management. Then let management decide how the communications go from there.

☐ **Leave on good terms.** In the future, you might want to come back and work at the firm—or you might have an opportunity to work with some of your former colleagues. You will have those opportunities only if you leave on good terms.

☐ **Give appropriate notice, and finish or hand off projects in an orderly way.**

☐ **Let the firm decide how to announce your departure.** If the firm allows you to send out a message, let the firm review it beforehand.

☐ **Keep your message positive.** Even if you are leaving because you had a bad experience, focus on the positive and thank your colleagues. This is not a time to get even or send out snide messages like, "I enjoyed working with *many* of you." Your stated reasons for leaving should focus on the positive aspects of your new position rather than any negative aspects of your current job.

☐ **Don't contradict firm management.** The firm will undoubtedly want to put the best face on your departure. Don't say anything that would contradict the "party line." Lots of people will want to know the "scoop" or the "real" reason you are leaving. Avoid that temptation. If you reveal information that is different from what management communicated, it will spread like wildfire. That will make management appear uninformed—or out of touch—not something that will endear you to the powers that be.

Special Advice If You Are Laid Off

Here is additional advice to consider if you are laid off:

☐ Again, do not burn bridges. Apart from some brief satisfaction, there is no point in taking parting shots. It is possible you will find that being laid off leads to opportunities you never would have had otherwise.

☐ Try not to take the situation personally. Many factors play a role in layoffs, particularly economics.

☐ Keep your emotions in check. A blow-up or meltdown is likely to confirm in the minds of some attorneys that they made the right decision.

☐ Do not commit to any terms of your separation on the spot.

☐ Ask whether the firm will provide outplacement services.

☐ Ask whether the firm is proposing any severance benefits and then find out what is typical in your market. Severance is often negotiable, but often also involves a release of liability.

☐ Ask for frank feedback about what (if anything) you could have done better.

☐ Figure out who might be willing to give you a good reference, and ask those people.

☐ Offer to do a first draft of a reference letter to save them time (and to help ensure it says what you want it to).

☐ Ask your employer to let you know about potential job opportunities.

☐ Ask your employer to keep you in mind for contract opportunities in the future.

☐ If you learn that you are going to be laid off at some future date, start looking for other jobs immediately. Do not expect the firm to change its mind based on last-minute miracles that you may perform or a sudden reversal in the firm's economic fortunes.

APPENDIX A

QUICK TIPS FOR SUCCESS

The Really Quick List:

Here is a very quick list of things to keep in mind to support your success. More detailed tips follow:

- ☐ Treat everyone with respect.
- ☐ Be pleasant, even when things are stressful.
- ☐ Work hard without complaint.
- ☐ Double check your work and never guess.
- ☐ Ask for feedback and follow the advice you receive.
- ☐ Listen and use every opportunity to learn.
- ☐ Develop a skill that others don't have and be assertive enough to tell other lawyers.
- ☐ Regularly think of things you can do to be helpful.
- ☐ Make a name for yourself writing articles for the firm's newsletters or blogs.

Building Relationships at the Office

- ☐ Try to make yourself indispensable, and try to anticipate other lawyers' needs.
- ☐ Be dependable.
- ☐ Ask other lawyers about the skills they think you should develop.
- ☐ Ask for feedback on your work.
- ☐ Work to enhance your skills.

☐ Don't be afraid to ask questions if you cannot figure out the answer.

☐ Make sure you understand the senior lawyers' expectations.

☐ Be respectful and good natured in the office.

☐ Don't contradict your colleagues in front of other lawyers or clients.

☐ Thank people.

☐ Remember birthdays.

☐ Attend firm social events.

☐ Don't get drunk at firm social events.

☐ Avoid all office romances.

☐ Be a superstar with electronic research software and other technology.

☐ Meet your billable-hours requirements.

Researching and Drafting

☐ Take advantage of services that will send you new cases and legal developments in your practice area by e-mail.

☐ Use firm resources such as librarians and the firm intranet.

☐ Double-check everything.

☐ Read cases in their entirety—not just head notes.

☐ Flag anything you come across in your research that may be problematic to your client's position, and try to come up with a solution to the problem.

☐ Take a legal writing seminar.

☐ Learn the meaning of every provision in your documents.

Practice Management

☐ Make sure you understand the assignment—and write it down.

☐ During discussions on a project, write down who is supposed to do what, and go over the list at the end of the conversation so that there are no misunderstandings.

☐ Never guess; look up everything.

☐ Complete projects before the absolute deadline.

☐ Write neatly to reduce errors in edits that others make for you.

☐ Get papers off your desk unless you are actively using them.

☐ If you do keep papers on your desk, make copies and file the originals.

☐ Keep papers and computer equipment away from your food and beverages and vice versa.

☐ Carefully proofread your documents before giving them to the senior lawyer or the client.

☐ Keep a record of all important conversations and the transmittal of all documents.

☐ Remember that clients and other lawyers may lose documents that you give them—plan accordingly.

☐ Review and organize files as soon as a matter is complete or winding down.

☐ If someone puts you on speakerphone, ask who is in the room so that you don't say anything inappropriate (such as communicating privileged information when non-clients are on the call).

☐ If there is something you need to be happier and more productive, ask.

☐ Do substantive work during your best hours of the day.

☐ Don't gossip.

☐ If you are asked to do something that you think is unethical, check with the appropriate person at your firm. You are responsible for your career, and even your current job is not worth your whole career.

☐ Don't try to change the firm—learn how to practice law.

Client Relations

☐ Be responsive and keep the client informed of your progress on a project.

☐ Listen.

☐ Spell and pronounce the client's name correctly.

☐ Make sure you know who the client is—and learn about the client's business.

☐ Find out the gender of the person with whom you will be communicating.

☐ Start out your answers to client's questions being as direct, definitive, and concise as possible. You can elaborate later in the conversation.

☐ Keep track of the people you have called so that if they call you back several days later, you'll know why you called them.

☐ Put a note on your phone or other reminder to change your "out of office" voicemail message.

☐ Stay out of the business deal—unless the terms of the deal have legal implications.

☐ Schedule times to return phone calls to clients to prevent phone tag.

☐ Don't make small mistakes; that will cause clients to assume that you make big ones.

☐ Take the initiative to assist strangers in the office who seem to be clueless.

APPENDIX B

A DOZEN PERSONAS TO AVOID

Here are a dozen traits to avoid as a new associate (or even a senior lawyer):

- [ ] **The Disorganized Associate.** This is the associate who is always losing things, causing unnecessary stress for everyone.

- [ ] **The Gossip.** This is the associate who can't keep his mouth shut. That makes other lawyers decide he can't keep their clients' confidences. It's also very unattractive.

- [ ] **The Grump.** This is the associate who constantly complains. The trait will make other lawyers conclude you would be happier elsewhere.

- [ ] **The Luncher.** This is the associate who is more interested in the law firm's perks than in working to pay for them.

- [ ] **The Name–Dropper.** This is the associate who lets everyone know all of the important people he knows. No one cares.

- [ ] **The Panicky Associate.** This is the associate who becomes paralyzed under pressure. If this is in your personality, fix it fast.

- [ ] **The Procrastinator.** This is the associate who lurches from crisis to crisis because of her own delay. This is another bad habit you need to fix fast.

- [ ] **The Schmoozer.** This associate spends most of his time being chummy. Yet another very unattractive trait.

☐   **The Show–Off.** This is the associate who constantly brags about how smart she is or how many hours she is billing. She implies that everyone else is dumb or lazy. This breeds contempt and loathing among peers and staff.

☐   **The Under–Deliverer.** This is the associate who always takes on too much work and then returns inferior or late projects.

☐   **The Union Leader.** This is the associate who swoops into the firm and immediately starts organizing the associates to petition the firm for change.

☐   **The Unkempt Associate.** This is the associate who looks like he just survived a ship-wreck. If you look disheveled, people may assume you are sloppy in general. Keep up appearances.

ACKNOWLEDGMENTS

From my star editor, D. Michelle Adkerson, to my agent, Penny Nelson, friends who nudged and nudged me to keep writing, to Greg in Costa Rica who came up with the title, and to Jason Stone who was miraculous with web design, the help and encouragement I have received for this book have been profoundly humbling.

Foster Pepper PLLC deserves special acknowledgment. I started my career at Foster Pepper and never once considered working at another firm.

I also owe a special debt of gratitude to Rita Alli at Stoel Rives LLP. Rita was incredibly supportive throughout the process, even though she had never even met me before I approached her about this book. And time and again, I called on Seann Hallisky and Wendy Werner, and they came through every time. My sister, Sarah Cleveland, also deserves special mention.

Finally, this book would not have happened without all the help and support from Staci Herr, Roxanne Birkel, and Joanne Fleming at Thomson Reuters, as well as the dozens of lawyers who generously gave their time to provide comments, advice, and war stories.

Just a few of the many people who have helped me with this project are listed below. I am extremely grateful.

- [ ] Alex Wagner
- [ ] Alice Ostdiek
- [ ] Allen D. Israel
- [ ] Allison Schwartzman
- [ ] Andrew Kamins
- [ ] Andrew Sachs
- [ ] Barbara Lynn Pedersen
- [ ] Ben Danis
- [ ] Cathy Johnson
- [ ] Chris Erker
- [ ] Chris Pepin
- [ ] Christopher Zachar
- [ ] David Buchholz
- [ ] Dave Horn

- [ ] Derek Wright
- [ ] Don Anderson
- [ ] Don Botts
- [ ] Emily Stubbs
- [ ] Foster Pepper PLLC
- [ ] Fred Parham
- [ ] Gregg Rodgers
- [ ] Isaac Ruiz
- [ ] J.D. Fugate
- [ ] James Puckett
- [ ] Jamie Pedersen
- [ ] Jason Stone
- [ ] Joanne Fleming
- [ ] John Stanley
- [ ] Jon Schneider
- [ ] Karen Reed
- [ ] Ken Leppert Jr.
- [ ] Kim Turner
- [ ] Kimberly Harris
- [ ] Kristen Gestaut
- [ ] Kyle Branum
- [ ] Lori Nomura
- [ ] Lori Salzarulo
- [ ] Marcia Cleveland
- [ ] Mark Alstead
- [ ] Mark Nielsen
- [ ] Mary Carolyn Boothby
- [ ] Matt Cohen
- [ ] Melford Cleveland
- [ ] Michael Gotham
- [ ] Michael J. Epstein
- [ ] Michelle Adkerson
- [ ] Mike Schechter
- [ ] Nicholas L. Smith
- [ ] Pam Bissonnette
- [ ] Patrick McNierney
- [ ] Penny Nelson
- [ ] Richard Wood
- [ ] Rita Alli
- [ ] Rob Castro
- [ ] Rob Lehman
- [ ] Rod Dembowski
- [ ] Roxanne Birkel
- [ ] Sam Castic
- [ ] Sarah Cleveland
- [ ] Seann Hallisky
- [ ] Spencer Cotton
- [ ] Susan Bannier
- [ ] Staci Herr
- [ ] Stephen Teply
- [ ] Stefan Mallen
- [ ] Steve DiJulio
- [ ] Struan Robertson
- [ ] Sydney Sigman
- [ ] Wade Harman
- [ ] Wendy L. Werner

CREDITS

"The Million Dollar Comma" excerpt is copyright Pinsent Masons LLP and has been reproduced with the firm's permission from OUT–LAW.COM, 26 October 2006. OUT–LAW.COM is part of Pinsent Masons LLP.

Numerous practice tips on confidentiality, client service, making a good impression, and other topics were excerpted with permission from *Ten Hints for New Lawyers: Some Things Which Would Be Important to Me if I Were a Client, Common and Uncommon Courtesies and Other Things to Think About in Your New Law Career,* by Allen D. Israel, Member, Foster Pepper PLLC, Seattle WA.

American Bar Association Formal Opinion 93–379, Billing for Professional Fees, Disbursements, and Other Expenses, December 6, 1993, © 1993 by the American Bar Association. All rights reserved. Excerpt reprinted by permission.

"A Dozen Personas to Avoid" adapted and reproduced with permission of Isaac Ruiz, attorney at law, Seattle, Washington.

INDEX

145

†